JAMES MᶜNAIR's
STEWS
& CASSEROLES

Photography by James McNair

Chronicle Books • San Francisco

Printed in Japan

Library of Congress
Cataloging-in-Publication Data
McNair, James K.
[Stews & casseroles]
James McNair's stews & casseroles/
photography by James McNair
p. cm.
ISBN 0-8118-0081-4 (hardcover)
1. Stews
2. Casserole cookery
I. Title
II. Title: James McNair's stews and casseroles
III. Title: Stews & casseroles
TX693.M36 1991
641.8'21—dc20   91-46246
                                          CIP

Distributed in Canada by
Raincoast Books
112 East Third Avenue
Vancouver, British Columbia V5T 1C8

10 9 8 7 6 5 4 3 2 1

Chronicle Books
275 Fifth Street
San Francisco, California 94103

For three dear friends—John Carr, Larry Heller, and Felix Wiench—with
gratitude for the dedication and tenderness with which they cared for Lin
Cotton's physical needs during his final months. This shared experience
bonded the four of us together in a lasting and loving relationship.

And in memory of my partner, best friend, and soulmate, Lin Cotton, and
our faithful dog, Buster Booroo. Lin and Buster were the finest companions
one could ever hope to find in life. They both left this existence on August
21, 1991, to run together freely in eternal sunshine. I will always love these
two whose lives and spirits are so entwined with mine.

Produced by The Rockpile Press, San Francisco and Lake Tahoe

**Art direction, photographic and food styling, and book design
by James McNair**

Editorial, styling, and photographic assistance by Ellen Berger-Quan

Kitchen assistance by Diane Quan

**Typography and mechanical production by Cleve Gallat of
CTA Graphics**

CONTENTS

INTRODUCTION

There is *adobo* from the Philippines, *tagine* from Morocco, *spezzatino* and *ossobucco* from Italy, and *stufato* from Greece. No matter what the language, such succulent and comforting dishes created through long, slow cooking are beloved around the world.

To English-speaking cooks, the term *stew* identifies a wide variety of dishes. In its broadest application, a stew is any dish in which small pieces of meat, poultry, fish, and/or vegetables are usually first browned in a little fat and then combined with seasonings and some liquid, tightly covered, and simmered gently until meltingly tender.

French chefs term these preparations a *ragout,* a word that originally described only stews made of meat, vegetables, and wine, but which now refers to any stew. They break down ragouts into several types, such as *fricassee* (a stew bound together with a creamy sauce), etouffée (a stew cooked, or "smothered," in its own juice), *navarin* (a lamb stew that is browned before cooking), *blanquette* (an unbrowned or white stew that is enriched and thickened with egg yolks and/or cream and usually flavored with lemon juice), and *casserole* (a stew simmered in a glazed earthenware pot).

In fact, the term *casserole* comes from the glazed earthenware dish in which food is slowly cooked on top of the stove or, more commonly, in an oven. In classic French cooking, the word *casserole* is often used interchangeably with *ragout.* Both terms refer to the process of extremely slow cooking in a covered heatproof dish.

In America we've split the terms. We think of stews as dishes containing bite-sized ingredients simmered in a covered pot, either on the stovetop or in an oven (when larger cuts of meat are cooked in the same manner, this method is known as braising and includes American pot roast and French *daube).* The word *casserole,* in contrast, has come to be used in association with dishes whose ingredients are partially cooked, then combined in a baking dish and finished in the oven. Unfortunately, casseroles have gained something of a bad reputation because of the days when convenience foods were all dumped together and baked into a mushy mass.

Both stews and casseroles are among our favorite comfort foods; they remind us of home and simpler times. Each can be prepared from inexpensive ingredients. Stewing, for example, is an excellent method for cooking the tougher cuts of meat, as the long, slow cooking breaks down the connective tissue, resulting in very tender meat. Another advantage is that most stews and casseroles can be made ahead and reheated. Nutrients are conserved, as the cooking liquid is eaten along with the dish.

Stews and casseroles are great one-dish main courses, making them easy meals for simple entertaining and terrific additions to a buffet table. To turn a stew into a meal, add a starchy accompaniment such as rice, polenta, potatoes, noodles, dumplings, croutons, baked savory pastry toppings, or good crusty bread. Casseroles often have the starch baked right in the dish. Serve a salad before, alongside, or after the stew or casserole and end with fresh fruit for an easy and nutritious meal. Of course, the simplicity of stews and casseroles also allows for splurging on a big gooey sweet for dessert. When choosing wine to serve with stews simmered with wine, be sure to stay with the same vintage for drinking that was used in the cooking.

I've divided this book into two sections, *stews* and *casseroles,* although in the true sense of the term, any of the stews may also be called casseroles if they are simmered in an earthenware dish. For practical purposes, I've included under casseroles those dishes that are partially cooked, then combined with other ingredients and baked in an oven. Most casseroles are fairly easy and straightforward. Just start with the finest and freshest ingredients available and follow the recipes for success. Although simple to cook, stews can prove a bit tricky, so the next two pages offer guidelines that might prove helpful.

Tips for Successful Stews

CHOOSING STEW POTS AND CASSEROLES

No matter whether you choose cast iron, enamelware, heavy-gauge aluminum, copper, or glazed earthenware, a pot for stewing should be heavy enough to distribute the low heat evenly and prevent sticking during the long cooking time. It should be both flame resistant and ovenproof, since it may be used on top of the stove and in the oven.

A dutch oven makes a great stew pot because of its shape and weight. Avoid those made of cast iron, however, when you are making a white stew such as a *blanquette* or a stew containing coconut milk; the iron will add an unappealing grayish tint to these white stews.

No matter what vessel is chosen, a tight-fitting lid should be used to reduce the loss of liquid from evaporation during the slow cooking. When in doubt about the fit of the lid, place a sheet of aluminum foil or baking parchment over the pot before adding the cover.

Glazed earthenware is traditional for casseroles and comes in a variety of sizes and shapes, including rounds, ovals, rectangles, and squares. Oven-tempered glass is a common and perfectly acceptable substitute.

SHOPPING. As with any good cooking, choose fresh, high-quality ingredients. The end results are only as good as what you start with. When purchasing meat for stews, tell the butcher what you are cooking and ask for suggestions as to which cut is best that day. Although less expensive, less desirable cuts can become quite tender when stewed and may actually have better flavor, I often choose a better cut that contains less fat and therefore fewer calories and less waste. The more tender cuts also require less cooking time.

PREPARING. Vegetables for stews should be cut to uniform size to ensure even cooking. In each of my recipes for meat stews, I suggest rinsing the meat under running cold water before cooking to remove any surface bacteria that can contribute an off-taste; these can develop quickly on small pieces of meat brought home from a butcher, especially when you purchase prewrapped packages and have no idea of when the meat was cut. If you cut your own cubes from a large piece of meat, the meat should be rinsed first and patted dry, then cut as directed in the recipe.

BROWNING. Meat browns best if it is very dry when it is added to the hot fat. If it has been rinsed or marinated, pat each piece dry with paper toweling before browning. Meat needs room to brown evenly and keep the heat uniformly distributed; brown the meat in batches to avoid crowding the pan. If it is necessary to add a bit more fat between batches, be sure to allow the fat to heat up before adding the meat; hot fat sears the meat and assures that less of the fat will be absorbed.

Although most stews begin with browning the major ingredients, some do not. A *blanquette,* or white stew, begins with only a brief searing of poultry, lamb, veal, or sweetbreads. The *tagines* of Morocco also traditionally skip the browning step.

STOVETOP OR OVEN? Although stews generally start out over direct heat, they may be finished by simmering either on top of the stove or in an oven. My recipes specify a method of cooking that seems most suitable to that particular dish, but feel free to choose the alternative cooking method. To cook a stew in the oven, transfer it to a preheated 350° F oven at the point where a recipe directs you to lower the heat to a simmer. Cooking time is about the same.

Boiling toughens meat. For tender meat, it is important to keep the temperature adjusted to maintain a very gentle simmer. When cooking on the range, keep the heat source low so that the temperature remains evenly distributed. The best oven temperature for stewing seems to be around 350° F;

check occasionally and adjust the heat to keep the dish simmering. Whether cooking in an oven or on a burner, a tight-fitting cover helps to maintain even temperature and to prevent evaporation of liquid. Even taking into account the considerable time required for cooking, stews and casseroles are fuel efficient due to the low heat used throughout the process.

I've tried stewing in the microwave, but the end results lack the complexity of flavors that I expect from stews. I have, however, started stew with help from the microwave, then simmered them conventionally to completion. For microwave stew techniques, see any of the excellent microwave cookbooks by Barbara Kafka.

THICKENING. Some stews are thickened by dredging the meat with flour before browning. Others call for sprinkling flour over the meat after browning or for adding it near the end of cooking. A few recipes call for making a roux of flour and oil that is added at the beginning or near the end of cooking. Still other stews are thickened simply by reducing the cooking liquid after the ingredients are tender, or by thickening the liquid with cream and/or egg yolk. A white stew that is thickened solely by the starch that comes from cooking potatoes in the dish is known as an Irish stew. Gumbo relies on either okra or filé to thicken slightly its tasty liquid.

DEGREASING. Depending upon the fat content of the meat, a finished stew may contain more fat than you would like. To degrease, remove the stew from the heat and cool slightly to allow fat to rise to the top, then draw strips of paper toweling across the top of the stew until most of the clear fat is collected on the paper. Alternatively, cook the stew several hours or a day ahead, cool almost to room temperature, cover, and refrigerate until cold. Before reheating, spoon off the layer of fat that rises to the top.

REHEATING. Many stews taste best when made a day before serving; this allows flavors to mellow and blend. Remove them from the heat, cool to room temperature, cover, and refrigerate. Gently reheat before serving. This practice is not advisable for stews containing fish or shellfish, although those stews can be prepared up to the point of adding the seafood, then cooled and refrigerated. Shortly before serving, reheat the stew base, add the fish, and finish cooking the stew. Likewise, stews calling for crisp vegetables, fresh herbs, cream, egg yolks, or other thickeners that are added just before serving can be cooked up to the point where these ingredients go in the pot. Refrigerate the stew and then gently reheat before adding the final ingredients.

SERVING

Stews should be ladled into shallow bowls or deep plates, preferably warmed. I photographed the stews in this book on classic French porcelain plates that are a cross between a bowl and a plate. They are standard tableware in bistros, where I've enjoyed some great stews.

Although stews are usually eaten with a fork, those with a lot of gravy or liquid should be served with spoons. Gumbo and most other seafood stews are always eaten with a spoon.

STEWS

Summer Garden Stew

Juice of 1 lemon (if using fresh artichokes)

12 small artichokes (about 2 ounces *each*), or 2 cups thawed frozen artichoke hearts

1 cup shelled fresh young fava beans or broad beans (about 10 ounces unshelled beans)

3 tablespoons plus ¼ cup light olive oil

18 green onions, white and pale green portions only

1 golden sweet pepper, stemmed, seeded, deveined, and cut into small squares

10 ounces whole baby carrots, peeled

8 ounces young green beans, trimmed

8 ounces asparagus, trimmed and cut on the diagonal into 2-inch lengths

1 cup dry white wine

1 cup homemade vegetable stock or chicken stock, reconstituted vegetable bouillon, or canned chicken broth, preferably low-sodium type

About 1 teaspoon salt

About 1 teaspoon freshly ground white pepper

¼ cup (½ stick) unsalted butter

1 tablespoon minced or pressed garlic, or to taste (optional)

2 cups French bread cubes, preferably day-old bread cut into ¾-inch cubes

12 ounces cherry tomatoes, stemmed

1 cup shelled green peas (about 1 pound unshelled)

About ½ cup mixed fresh herb sprigs such as savory or tarragon and/or small herb leaves such as mint or basil

Pesticide-free edible flowers such as nasturtiums for garnish

Vary the ingredients in this stew according to what vegetables are in abundance in the market or in your garden.

If using fresh artichokes, fill a large bowl with water and add the lemon juice. Pull off and discard all the tough outer, dark green leaves from the artichokes. Cut off and discard the stems and the top half of each artichoke. With a small, sharp knife, trim away any portion of the dark green leaves that remains. As each artichoke heart is trimmed, drop it into the water to prevent darkening. Set aside. If using thawed artichokes, set aside.

Bring a small pot of water to a boil over high heat. Drop in the fava beans and parboil for 3 to 4 minutes. Drain. Peel off and discard the thin layer of skin from each bean. Set the beans aside.

Drain the artichokes. In a heavy stew pot such as a dutch oven, heat the 3 tablespoons oil over medium-high heat. Add the onions, sweet pepper, carrots, and artichokes and sauté for about 3 minutes. Add the green beans, asparagus, and reserved fava beans and sauté for about 5 minutes longer. Stir in the wine and stock, bouillon, or broth and bring to a boil. Season to taste with salt and pepper. Reduce the heat to low, cover tightly, and simmer, stirring occasionally, until the vegetables are tender and very little liquid remains, about 1 hour.

Meanwhile, in a large sauté pan or skillet, melt the butter with the remaining ¼ cup oil over medium-low heat. Add the garlic (if used) and bread and toss until the bread pieces are evenly coated. Reduce the heat to low (or transfer to a preheated 350° F oven) and cook, stirring or turning frequently, until the bread is golden on all sides, about 20 minutes. Transfer the bread to paper toweling to drain and cool slightly.

About 10 minutes before serving the stew, stir in the tomatoes and peas and simmer to heat through. Taste and adjust the seasonings.

Scatter each portion of stew with the bread cubes and herbs sprigs and/or leaves. Garnish with flowers.

SERVES 6.

Ratatouille Provençale

3 red or golden sweet peppers
¾ cup plus 2 tablespoons fruity olive oil,
　preferably extra-virgin
2 cups sliced yellow onion
2 tablespoons coarsely chopped garlic
1 pound eggplant, cut into ¾-inch cubes
2 pounds zucchini, sliced about ¼ inch
　thick
6 cups peeled, seeded, and chopped fresh
　or drained canned plum tomatoes
　(about 3 pounds)
1 tablespoon minced mixed fresh bay leaf,
　lavender, oregano, rosemary, summer
　savory, and thyme, in equal portions,
　or 1 teaspoon crumbled dried *herbes
　de Provence*
About 1 teaspoon sugar
Salt
Freshly ground black pepper
⅓ cup chopped fresh basil
Pesticide-free lavender blossoms for
　garnish (optional)
Lavender foliage for garnish (optional)

When cooked separately, then tossed together for a final blending, each vegetable in this Mediterranean favorite retains its characteristic flavor. Excellent with roasted or grilled chicken or lamb.

Place the peppers on a grill rack over a charcoal fire, hold them over a gas flame, or place them under a preheated broiler. Roast, turning several times, until the skin is charred on all sides. Place them in a loosely closed paper bag to cool for about 10 to 15 minutes. Remove from the bag and rub away the charred skin with your fingertips. Cut the peppers in half and remove and discard the stems, seeds, and veins. Slice lengthwise into long, thin strips and set aside.

In a sauté pan or heavy stew pot such as a dutch oven, heat ¼ cup of the oil over medium-high heat. Add the onion and sauté until soft and golden, about 8 minutes. Add the garlic and reserved pepper strips and sauté for 1 minute longer. Transfer the vegetables to a colander set over a bowl; discard the oil that collects in the bowl.

Heat ¼ cup of the remaining oil in the same pan. Add the eggplant and sauté until lightly browned, about 8 minutes. Add to the colander with the onion mixture.

Heat ¼ cup of the remaining oil in the same pan. Add the zucchini and sauté until lightly browned, about 8 minutes. Add to the draining vegetables.

Heat the remaining 2 tablespoons oil in the same pan. Add the tomatoes, minced or crumbled herbs, and sugar to taste and bring to a boil. Stir in the sautéed vegetables and season to taste with salt and pepper. Return the mixture to a boil, then reduce the heat to low, cover, and simmer, stirring occasionally, until all the vegetables are very tender but still hold their shapes, about 30 minutes. Just before serving, stir in the chopped basil.

Sprinkle each portion with lavender blossoms (if used) and garnish with lavender foliage (if used).

SERVES 8 AS AN ACCOMPANIMENT, OR 4 AS A MAIN DISH.

Thai Vegetable Curry

Thai Green Curry Paste (page 92)
2 tablespoons high-quality vegetable oil
3 cups canned coconut milk
3 tablespoons fish sauce, or 1 tablespoon
  soy sauce
1 pound boiling potatoes, peeled and then
  halved or quartered if large
1 pound slender Asian eggplants, cut into
  1-inch-thick slices, or 1 pound globe
  eggplants, cut into 1-inch dice
12 ounces baby carrots, left whole, or
  larger carrots, cut into 1½-inch
  lengths
2 cups broccoli florets (from about
  1 pound)
3 to 4 ounces small green beans, left
  whole, or larger green beans, cut into
  3-inch lengths
½ cup chopped fresh cilantro (coriander)
Minced red sweet pepper or red hot chile
  for garnish
Minced fresh cilantro (coriander) for
  garnish
Garlic flowers (sometimes sold as garlic
  pearls) for garnish (optional)

Spicy Thai curry pastes—definitely not for the fainthearted—are available in cans at stores that specialize in Southeast Asian foods, although freshly made paste has better flavor. You won't need all of the paste for this recipe, but it keeps for several weeks in the refrigerator. Use the remainder in soups, pasta sauces, marinades, or other spicy dishes, or make this satisfying curry again.

Serve this coconut-rich stew with fluffy rice, preferably the jasmine type imported from Thailand.

Prepare the curry paste and set aside.

In a nonreactive sauté pan or heavy stew pot such as a dutch oven (avoid using cast iron, which turns the coconut milk gray), heat the oil over medium heat. Add about ¼ cup of the curry paste, or to taste, and cook 2 to 3 minutes. Stir in the coconut milk and fish sauce or soy sauce and simmer for about 5 minutes.

Add the potatoes, eggplants, and carrots and bring to a boil. Reduce the heat to low and simmer for 10 minutes. Add the broccoli and green beans and simmer until all of the vegetables are done to preference, about 10 minutes longer. Just before serving, stir in the chopped cilantro and heat through.

Sprinkle each portion with minced pepper and minced cilantro. Garnish with garlic flowers (if used).

SERVES 6.

Pueblo Winter Vegetable Stew

1 cup dried beans such as Anasazi or pinto
Water, stock, or broth to cover beans
1 bay leaf
1½ teaspoons cumin seed
2 tablespoons chile powder, preferably
    from ancho or pasilla chiles
2 tablespoons minced fresh oregano, or
    2 teaspoons crumbled dried oregano
¼ teaspoon ground cinnamon
¼ cup canola oil or other
    high-quality vegetable oil
1½ cups chopped yellow onion
1 tablespoon minced hot chile
1 teaspoon minced or pressed garlic
2 cups peeled, seeded, and chopped fresh
    or drained canned plum tomatoes
    (about 1 pound)
About 3 cups homemade vegetable stock,
    reconstituted vegetable bouillon, or
    chicken broth, preferably low-sodium
    type
About 1¾ pounds winter squash such as
    'Buttercup,' 'Butternut,' or 'Golden
    Nugget,' peeled, seeded, and cut into
    1-inch cubes (enough to equal 4 cups)
2 cups freshly cut or thawed frozen corn
    kernels (from about 4 medium-sized
    ears)
½ cup chopped fresh cilantro (coriander)
    or parsley
½ cup pine nuts
Fresh cilantro or parsley sprigs for
    garnish

If you wish to serve this Native American-inspired stew in a squash shell such as the 'Golden Nugget' variety shown here, pierce the shells in several places with the tines of a fork or a small, sharp knife. Place the squash in a shallow baking pan and add water to the pan to a depth of ¼ inch. Bake in a preheated 400° F oven until the squash is tender, 30 to 40 minutes. Remove from the oven. Wearing oven mitts, position the squash on a cutting surface and cut off the tops. Using a spoon, scrape out and discard the seeds and stringy portions from the squash. Carefully peel off and discard the skin, if desired.

Carefully pick over the beans to remove any shriveled beans and foreign matter. Place in a bowl, cover with cold water, and let stand overnight. Drain the beans and transfer to a deep saucepan with water, stock, or broth to cover by about 1 inch. Add the bay leaf and bring the beans to a boil over high heat. Reduce the heat to low, cover, and simmer until the beans are tender, 45 minutes to 1½ hours, depending upon the type of bean used. Drain the beans, reserving the cooking liquid. Set the beans and liquid aside.

In a small, heavy dry skillet, heat the cumin seed over medium heat, stirring or shaking the pan quite frequently, until fragrant, 2 to 3 minutes. Be careful not to burn the seed. Pour the seed onto a plate to cool, then grind to a powder in an electric spice grinder. Combine the ground seed, chile powder, oregano, and cinnamon in a small bowl and set aside.

In a sauté pan or heavy stew pot such as a dutch oven, heat the oil over medium-high heat. Add the onion and sauté until the onion is soft but not browned, about 5 minutes. Add the minced chile, garlic, and reserved spice mixture and sauté for 1 minute longer. Add the tomatoes and ½ cup of the stock, bouillon, or broth. Bring to a boil, then reduce the heat to medium and simmer for about 5 minutes.

Add the squash and about 2 cups of the stock, bouillon, or broth and cook until the squash is slightly soft when pierced with a small, sharp knife or wooden skewer, about 10 minutes. Stir in the reserved beans and the corn and cook until the squash is tender, about 10 minutes, adding more stock, bouillon, broth, or reserved bean liquid if the stew gets too dry. A few minutes before serving, stir in the chopped herb.

Meanwhile, pour the pine nuts into a small, heavy skillet and place over medium heat. Cook, stirring or shaking the pan frequently, until the nuts are lightly toasted, about 5 minutes. Pour onto a plate to cool.

Sprinkle pine nuts over each portion and garnish with herb sprigs.
SERVES 6.

Vegetable Pot Pie with Spicy Pastry

Spicy Cream Cheese Pastry (page 92),
   double recipe if making individual pies

WINTER VEGETABLE RAGOUT
6 tablespoons (¾ stick) unsalted butter
3 tablespoons canola oil or other
   high-quality vegetable oil
2 cups chopped leeks, white and pale
   green portions only
1 cup thinly sliced fennel
2 teaspoons minced or pressed garlic
12 ounces carrots, peeled and cut into
   matchsticks (about 2 cups)
12 ounces rutabagas or turnips, peeled
   and cut into matchsticks (about
   2 cups)
12 ounces parsnips, peeled and cut into
   matchsticks (about 2 cups)
12 ounces sweet potatoes (not yam
   varieties), peeled and cut into
   matchsticks (about 2 cups)
¼ cup chopped fresh parsley, summer
   savory, or tarragon
½ cup dry white wine
About 2 cups homemade vegetable stock
   or chicken stock, reconstituted
   vegetable bouillon, or canned chicken
   broth, preferably low-sodium type
2 tablespoons all-purpose flour
½ cup half and half

1 egg white, beaten, for moistening
1 egg yolk beaten with 1 tablespoon
   heavy (whipping) cream for glaze
Pesticide-free honeysuckle blossoms for
   garnish (optional)

Old-fashioned pot pies are actually stews topped with a pastry crust. If you wish to turn this into a chicken or turkey pot pie, brown bite-sized pieces of boned chicken or turkey in the butter and oil and remove to a bowl before adding the vegetables. Return the fowl to the pot before adding the wine and stock and cook until the meat is tender. The vegetable ragout may also be served on its own without the crust.

Prepare the pastry and chill.

To make the ragout, melt 3 tablespoons of the butter with the oil in a heavy stew pot such as a dutch oven over medium-high heat. Add the leeks and fennel and sauté until soft but not browned, about 3 minutes. Stir in the garlic, carrots, rutabagas or turnips, parsnips, potatoes, and about half of the herbs and sauté for about 3 minutes. Add the wine and stock, bouillon, or broth and bring to a boil. Reduce the heat to medium-low, cover, and simmer until the vegetables are tender, 15 to 20 minutes.

Strain the cooking liquid into a bowl and transfer the vegetables to a separate bowl. Melt the remaining 3 tablespoons of butter in the cooking pot. Add the flour and cook, whisking or stirring, for 3 minutes. Gradually whisk or stir in the cooking liquid and half and half. Simmer until the liquid is thickened to sauce consistency, about 5 minutes. Combine the sauce, vegetables, and the remaining herbs and spoon the mixture into a shallow 2-quart casserole or into 6 shallow baking dishes such as quiche dishes, measuring 5 to 6 inches in diameter. Cool slightly, then cover and refrigerate until quite cold.

On a lightly floured board, roll out the dough about ¼ inch thick. Using a ruler as a straight edge and a sharp knife or rolling pastry cutter, cut into long strips about ½ inch wide. Surround the edge of the dish with a strip of dough and pinch the edges to form a decorative pattern. Cut the dough strips to a length that will fit across the top of the casserole. Crisscross the dough strips to form a lattice design over the filling. Moisten the ends of each dough strip with beaten egg white and press together with the strip surrounding the dish edges. Pinch off any excess dough and smooth the edges with your fingers. Brush the top of the pastry with the egg glaze. Refrigerate for at least 30 minutes before cooking.

Alternatively, roll out the dough to fit the top of the baking dish, allowing for an overlap of about 1½ inches. Place the dough over the top of the dish and press with fingers to secure the edges to the baking dish. Refrigerate for at least 30 minutes before cooking.

Preheat an oven to 450° F. Bake the pie for 10 minutes, then reduce the heat to 350° F and continue baking until the crust is golden and crisp, 20 to 25 minutes.

Garnish each portion with honeysuckle (if used).

SERVES 6.

California Cioppino

¼ cup light olive oil
½ cup chopped shallot
1 cup diced red sweet pepper
1 cup diced green sweet pepper
1 tablespoon minced or pressed garlic
1 teaspoon minced fresh ginger root
3 cups peeled, seeded, and chopped fresh
 or drained canned plum tomatoes
 (about 1½ pounds)
2 tablespoons tomato paste
¼ cup minced fresh parsley, preferably
 flat-leaf type
2 cups dry white wine
2 cups homemade fish stock, or
 2 cups canned chicken broth,
 preferably low-sodium type
About 1 teaspoon salt
About ½ teaspoon freshly ground black
 pepper
2 Dungeness crabs, disjointed and cracked
1½ pounds white firm-fleshed fish fillet,
 cut into chunks
8 ounces sea scallops
12 ounces shrimp, peeled and deveined
12 mussels in the shell, debearded and
 well scrubbed
12 clams in the shell, well scrubbed
¼ cup minced fresh basil, preferably Thai
 type, or cilantro (coriander)
3 tablespoons freshly squeezed lemon juice
Pesticide-free, nontoxic flowers such as
 cornflowers for garnish (optional)
Lemon wedges for serving
Tabasco sauce or other hot chile sauce for
 serving

Serve with plenty of crusty French bread, preferably sourdough, to soak up all of the flavorful liquid. If crabs are unavailable, substitute lobster.

In a heavy stew pot such as a dutch oven, heat the oil over medium heat. Add the shallot and red and green peppers and sauté until soft but not browned, about 5 minutes. Add the garlic and ginger root and sauté for 1 minute longer. Add the tomato, tomato paste, and about half of the parsley and cook for about 2 minutes.

Stir in 1 cup of the wine and the stock or broth. Season to taste with salt and pepper. Bring to a boil over medium heat, then reduce the heat to low and simmer for about 15 minutes.

Add the crab, cover, and simmer for about 10 minutes. Add the fish fillet and scallops, cover, and simmer for about 5 minutes longer. Add the shrimp, cover, and simmer until they turn bright pink and opaque, about 3 minutes.

Meanwhile, place the mussels and clams in a pot with the remaining 1 cup wine. Place over medium-high heat, cover, bring to a boil, and steam for 6 minutes (essential to kill any potentially harmful parasites). Strain the liquid into the pot with the seafood and then transfer the mussels and clams in their shells to the simmering stew as well, discarding any with shells that did not open. Stir in the basil or cilantro and lemon juice and heat through. Taste and correct the seasonings.

Garnish each portion with flowers (if used) and offer lemon wedges and Tabasco for seasoning the stew to taste at the table.
SERVES 6.

Curried Shellfish Stew

3 tablespoons high-quality vegetable oil
  or unsalted butter
1 cup chopped shallot or red onion
1 cup chopped golden or red sweet pepper
1 tablespoon Curry Powder (page 91) or
  high-quality commercial mild or hot
  curry powder, or to taste
1 teaspoon minced or pressed garlic
2 fresh hot chiles, preferably Scotch
  Bonnet, stemmed, seeded, deveined,
  and cut lengthwise into long, thin
  strips
1 cup homemade fish stock or chicken
  stock or canned chicken broth,
  preferably low-sodium type
1 cup canned coconut milk
4 tablespoons freshly squeezed lime juice
18 large shrimp, peeled and deveined if
  desired
1 pound scallops
12 mussels in the shell, debearded and
  well scrubbed
12 clams in the shell, well scrubbed
1 pound cooked lobster meat
3 tablespoons minced fresh cilantro
  (coriander)
2 tablespoons unsalted butter
Salt
Freshly ground black pepper
Minced fresh lime zest for garnish

Use any combination of fresh shellfish in this tropical island-inspired stew. Serve with Perfect Rice (page 87). A crisp vegetable salad of asparagus or green beans is a good accompaniment.

In a heavy, nonreactive stew pot such as a dutch oven (avoid cast iron, which will turn coconut milk gray), heat the oil or melt the butter over medium-low heat. Add the shallot or onion, sweet pepper, and curry powder and sauté until the vegetables are soft but not browned, 5 to 8 minutes. Stir in the garlic and chiles and sauté for about 1 minute.

Add the 1 cup stock or broth, coconut milk, and 2 tablespoons of the lime juice. Bring to a boil over medium-high heat. Reduce the heat to low, cover with a lid slightly ajar, and simmer for about 15 minutes.

Add the shrimp, scallops, mussels, and clams to the simmering coconut milk mixture. Cover and cook until the mussels and clams open and the shrimp and scallop meat is opaque, about 5 minutes. Discard any clams or mussels that do not open. Stir in the lobster meat, the remaining 2 tablespoons lime juice, cilantro, butter, and salt and pepper to taste. Reduce the heat to low and simmer, uncovered, until the butter melts and the lobster is heated through, about 3 minutes.

Sprinkle each portion with the lime zest.

SERVES 6.

Louisiana Gumbo

½ cup plus 2 tablespoons canola oil or
  other high-quality vegetable oil
½ cup all-purpose flour
1½ cups chopped yellow onion
1½ cups chopped celery
½ cup chopped green sweet pepper
½ cup chopped fresh parsley
1 teaspoon minced or pressed garlic
8 ounces okra, stemmed and sliced (if
  available)
4 cups homemade chicken stock or canned
  chicken broth, preferably low-sodium
  type
4 cups water
¼ cup Worcestershire sauce
¼ cup catsup
¼ teaspoon Tabasco sauce, or to taste
1 cup peeled, seeded, and chopped fresh or
  drained canned plum tomatoes (about
  ½ pound)
About 2 teaspoons salt
8 ounces flavorful baked ham, cut into
  small dice
1 bay leaf
1½ teaspoons *each* minced fresh thyme
  and rosemary, or
  ½ teaspoon *each* crumbled dried
  thyme and rosemary
¼ teaspoon crushed dried hot chile, or to
  taste
1 cup shredded cooked chicken
1 pound cooked crab meat, picked over
  for shell fragments and flaked
1½ pounds cooked shrimp, shelled and
  deveined
12 small oysters, freshly shucked, with
  liquor (optional)
About 1 tablespoon brown sugar
About 2 tablespoons freshly squeezed
  lemon juice
1½ teaspoons filé (if not using okra)
Minced fresh parsley for garnish

This is my all-time favorite gumbo recipe, which was originally given to me by Ruth Dosher, one of the best cooks in my hometown of Jonesville, Louisiana. Since making the roux is time-consuming, I always double the recipe so there will be plenty of gumbo for several days or for a party.

Most Louisiana gumbo cooks use *either* okra or filé (powdered sassafrass root), but never in combination. If okra is unavailable, use filé, which can be found in gourmet groceries and better supermarkets.

Ladle the gumbo into shallow bowls and top with a scoop of cooked white rice.

In a 4-quart stockpot over medium-low heat, warm ½ cup of the oil. Whisk in the flour. Stir frequently for the first 20 minutes, then stir constantly until the roux is very dark brown, about 25 minutes longer; do not burn!

Add the onion, celery, sweet pepper, chopped parsley, and garlic and cook, stirring frequently, until the vegetables are very soft, about 45 minutes.

Meanwhile, in a sauté pan or heavy skillet, heat the remaining 2 tablespoons oil over medium-high heat. Add the okra and sauté until lightly browned, 10 to 15 minutes. Transfer the okra to the stockpot.

Add the chicken stock or broth, water, Worcestershire sauce, catsup, Tabasco sauce, tomato, salt to taste, ham, bay leaf, thyme, rosemary, and chile. Bring to a boil, then reduce the heat to low, cover, and simmer for 3 to 4 hours, stirring occasionally.

About 30 minutes before serving, add the chicken, crab, and shrimp, and continue simmering. About 10 minutes before serving, stir in the oysters and their liquor (if used) and season to taste with sugar and lemon juice. If you have not used okra, remove the pot from the heat and stir in the filé. Taste and adjust seasonings.

Sprinkle each portion with parsley.

SERVES 6.

Crawfish Etouffée

12 tablespoons (¾ cup or 1½ sticks)
    unsalted butter
2 cups finely chopped yellow onion
½ cup finely chopped celery
½ cup chopped red or green sweet pepper
1 teaspoon minced or pressed garlic
1 cup crawfish cooking water, fish stock,
    chicken stock, or canned chicken
    broth, preferably low-sodium type
1 large firm ripe tomato, peeled, seeded,
    and chopped
1 tablespoon Worcestershire sauce
1 tablespoon Tabasco sauce, or to taste
2 pounds blanched, peeled crawfish tails
2 tablespoons crawfish fat
2 teaspoons sweet paprika, or as needed to
    achieve rich color
About ½ teaspoon salt
About ½ teaspoon freshly ground black
    pepper
½ cup finely chopped green onion
2 tablespoons minced fresh parsley
1 tablespoon freshly squeezed lemon juice
Cooked whole crawfish in the shell for
    garnish (optional)

In this southern Louisiana étouffée, a name that is taken from the French for "smothered," the crawfish are usually cooked in a seasoned broth made with water leftover from blanching the crawfish before peeling. When a roux or other thickening agent is added, the dish is called crawfish stew.

Fishmongers can procure Louisiana crawfish two ways: whole live ones or just the tails, which have been blanched and peeled. Peeled tails are infinitely easier to use and come either packed in ice (definitely the best flavor) or frozen; in either case a bag of yellowish fat from crawfish heads is usually included or may be purchased separately. Check gourmet magazine ads for current mail-order sources. Shrimp, lobster chunks, or crab meat may be substituted for or combined with the crawfish.

This delectable dish is traditionally served over fluffy white rice, but many cooks today spoon the rich crawfish over pasta.

In a heavy stew pot such as a dutch oven, melt 2 tablespoons of the butter over medium-low heat. Add the onion, celery, and sweet pepper and sauté until the vegetables are wilted but not browned, 5 to 8 minutes. Add the garlic and sauté for 1 minute longer. Add the cooking water, stock, or broth, tomato, Worcestershire sauce, and Tabasco sauce. Bring to a boil, then reduce the heat to low and simmer for about 20 minutes.

Add the remaining 10 tablespoons butter, 1 tablespoon at a time; stir only in one direction and do not add the next piece of butter until the previous one has completely melted.

When all of the butter has been added, stir in the crawfish tails, crawfish fat, and enough paprika to give the sauce a rich red hue, continuing to stir in the same direction. Cook, stirring frequently, until the crawfish is tender and the sauce is very creamy, about 12 minutes. Season to taste with salt and pepper. Stir in the green onion, parsley, and lemon juice.

Garnish each portion with the whole cooked crawfish (if used).
SERVES 6.

Chicken and White Wine Stew
(Coq au Vin Blanc)

1 stewing hen (4 to 5 pounds), cut into serving pieces, or about 4½ pounds chicken thighs, legs, and breasts
Salt
Freshly ground black pepper
5 ounces thickly sliced bacon
1 cup sliced yellow onion
1 teaspoon minced or pressed garlic, or to taste
1½ teaspoons minced fresh thyme, or ½ teaspoon crumbled dried thyme
1 bay leaf
3 cups dry white wine
2 cups homemade chicken stock or canned chicken broth, preferably low-sodium type
¼ cup (½ stick) unsalted butter
About 30 pearl onions
12 ounces small fresh mushrooms, preferably morels or other wild varieties, one type or a combination, or large mushrooms, cut into quarters or bite-sized pieces
2 tablespoons all-purpose flour blended with 2 tablespoons softened unsalted butter
Whole fresh chives for garnish

If you can locate a stewing hen, this white variation on a French red-wine stew will be exceptionally flavorful. Be sure to choose a good wine and serve the same vintage with the stew.

Quickly rinse the chicken under cold running water and pat dry with paper toweling. Season lightly with salt and pepper. Set aside.

In a large sauté pan, cook the bacon over medium heat until crisp. Using tongs, transfer the bacon to paper toweling to drain. Set aside.

Heat the bacon drippings over medium-high heat. Add as many of the chicken pieces as will fit comfortably without crowding and brown on all sides. Using tongs or a slotted utensil, transfer the browned chicken to paper toweling to drain. Brown the remaining chicken pieces in the same manner. Arrange the chicken in a heavy stew pot such as a dutch oven or a 3- or 4-quart casserole and set aside.

Preheat an oven to 350° F.

In the same pan used for browning the chicken, add the sliced onion and sauté over medium-high heat until soft and golden, about 8 minutes. Add the garlic, thyme, and bay leaf and sauté for 1 minute longer. Pour the mixture over the chicken. Pour the wine and stock or broth into the sauté pan and raise the heat to high. Bring to a boil, scraping all the browned bits from the bottom and sides of the pan. Pour over the chicken. Cover the stew pot tightly and cook in the oven, stirring several times, until the chicken is very tender when pierced with a small, sharp knife, 1½ to 2 hours.

Meanwhile, in a sauté pan or skillet, melt the butter over medium-high heat. Add the pearl onions and mushrooms and sauté until the onions are lightly colored, about 3 minutes. Set aside.

About 20 minutes before the chicken is ready, crumble the reserved bacon and stir it and the sautéed onions and mushrooms into the stew. Return to the oven until the chicken is tender.

Remove the stew from the oven. Strain the liquid into a saucepan and remove any fat that rises to the surface. Bring the liquid to a boil over high heat and cook until the liquid is reduced to about 3 cups. Whisk the butter-flour mixture into the sauce and place over medium heat. Cook, stirring or whisking continuously, until the sauce thickens slightly, about 5 minutes. Taste and correct seasonings. Return the chicken to the sauce and heat through.

Garnish each portion with the whole chives.

SERVES 6.

Brunswick Stew

5 to 6 pounds chicken, squirrel, and/or rabbit, cut into serving pieces
Salt
Freshly ground black pepper
About 3 tablespoons high-quality vegetable oil
About 3 tablespoons unsalted butter
2 cups sliced yellow onion
1 cup sliced celery
3 cups peeled, seeded, and chopped ripe or drained canned tomatoes (about 1½ pounds)
1 bay leaf
1 ham bone (about 2 pounds), preferably from a country-style ham (optional)
About 4 cups homemade chicken stock or canned chicken broth, preferably low-sodium type
Corn Dumplings (page 92; optional)
1 pound boiling potatoes, peeled and cut into ½-inch dice
3 or 4 medium-sized carrots, sliced or cut into ½-inch dice (optional)
3 cups freshly shelled or thawed frozen lima beans (about 1½ pounds unshelled)
2 cups freshly cut or thawed frozen corn kernels (from about 4 medium-sized ears)
Tabasco sauce or other hot chile sauce
Ground paprika or cayenne pepper
Whole fresh sage leaves or parsley sprigs for garnish

Although this Southern classic is traditionally made from squirrel or rabbit, or a combination of the two, an equally good stew can be made from chicken or a combination of light meats such as rabbit, veal, pork, and any poultry.

Quickly rinse the meat under cold running water and pat dry with paper toweling. Season to taste with salt and pepper.

In a heavy stew pot such as a dutch oven, heat 2 tablespoons of the oil and 2 tablespoons of the butter over medium-high heat until the butter melts. Add as many pieces of the meat as will fit comfortably without crowding and brown on all sides. Using tongs or a slotted utensil, transfer the browned meat to a plate. Brown the remaining meat in the same manner, adding butter and/or oil as necessary to prevent sticking.

To the same pot used for browning the meat, add enough oil and/or butter to that remaining in the pot to equal 2 tablespoons. Add the onion and celery and sauté until soft, about 5 minutes.

Return the meat to the pot. Add the tomato, bay leaf, ham bone (if used), and enough stock or broth to cover barely. Season to taste with salt and pepper and bring to a boil over medium-high heat. Reduce the heat to low, cover tightly, and simmer, stirring several times, until the meat is very tender, 45 minutes to 1 hour.

Using tongs or a slotted utensil, transfer the meat and the ham bone to a platter. Remove all meat from the bones, cut into bite-sized pieces, and set aside; discard the bones. Continue simmering the stew liquid, covered, for about 30 minutes.

Prepare the dumpling batter (if used) and set aside.

Add the potatoes, carrots (if used), and lima beans to the stew, cover partially, and simmer until the potatoes are almost tender when pierced with a small, sharp knife, 15 to 20 minutes longer. Stir in the boned meat and the corn. Taste and adjust seasonings, adding Tabasco sauce to taste.

Drop the dumpling batter on top of the simmering stew by the heaping tablespoonful. Cover tightly and simmer until the dumplings are puffy and a wooden skewer inserted in the center comes out clean, about 15 minutes.

Sprinkle each portion with paprika or cayenne and garnish with the herb leaves or sprigs.

SERVES 8.

Chicken Curry

8 boned and skinned chicken breast halves
2 tablespoons high-quality vegetable oil
3 tablespoons unsalted butter
Salt
Freshly ground black pepper
¾ cup chopped shallot
¼ cup Curry Powder (page 91) or
   commercial hot or mild high-quality
   curry powder, or to taste
1½ cups canned coconut milk
1½ cups homemade chicken stock or
   canned chicken broth, preferably
   low-sodium type
3 tablespoons all-purpose flour

CONDIMENTS
Shredded fresh or dried coconut
Coarsely chopped dry-roasted peanuts or
   cashews
Minced green onion
Chutney
Currants or raisins

Almost everyone enjoys an Indian curry. This version is simple and quickly made yet quite satisfying. Offer your guests plenty of hot cooked rice, preferably the delicately flavored basmati type, with this pleasantly robust dish.

Quickly rinse the chicken under cold running water and pat dry with paper toweling. Cut the breasts lengthwise into finger-wide strips. Sprinkle lightly with salt and pepper. Set aside.

In a sauté pan or heavy stew pot such as a dutch oven, melt the oil and 1 tablespoon of the butter over medium-high heat. Add as many of the chicken strips as will fit comfortably without overcrowding the pan and cook, turning frequently, until opaque all over. Using tongs or a slotted utensil, transfer the chicken to a plate. Cook the remaining chicken in the same manner.

Add the remaining 2 tablespoons butter to the pan and melt over medium-low heat. Add the shallot and curry powder and sauté until the shallot is soft, about 5 minutes. Sprinkle with the flour and sauté about 3 minutes longer.

Stir in the coconut milk and stock or broth and bring to a simmer. Return the chicken to the pan. Reduce the heat to low, cover, and simmer until the sauce thickens to the consistency of heavy (whipping) cream and the chicken is opaque all the way through when tested by cutting with a small, sharp knife at the thickest portion, about 10 minutes. Taste and correct the seasonings.

Offer the condiments at the table.

SERVES 8.

Deep South Duck Fricassee

3 wild ducks, whole or cut up, or 12 small
    boneless duck breasts
Salt
Freshly ground black or white pepper
About 8 tablespoons high-quality
    vegetable oil
¼ cup all-purpose flour
2 cups chopped yellow onion
1 teaspoon minced or pressed garlic
About 1½ cups homemade duck or
    chicken stock, canned chicken broth
    (preferably low-sodium type), or water
Minced green onion for garnish
Julienned fresh orange zest for garnish

This is the way my mother has always cooked the wild duck shot by Daddy. She then slices the meat and serves it along with the gravy over a huge platter of fluffy rice. I make the dish with domestic Muscovy duck breasts, although any duck could be used; better meat markets and some Asian poultry markets sell duck breasts and/or leg-and-thigh portions. It is delicious with Wild Rice Custards (page 90) as shown.

Quickly rinse the duck under cold running water and pat dry with paper toweling. Sprinkle lightly with salt and pepper.

In a heavy stew pot such as a dutch oven, heat 3 tablespoons of the oil over medium-high heat. Add as many of the duck pieces as will fit comfortably in the pan without crowding and brown on all sides. Using a slotted utensil or tongs, remove the duck to a plate. Brown the remaining duck in the same manner, adding more oil as necessary to prevent sticking.

To the same pot used for browning the duck, add enough oil to that remaining in the pot to equal about 3 tablespoons. Add the onion and sauté until soft and golden, about 8 minutes. Add the garlic and sauté for 1 minute longer.

Meanwhile, in a heavy skillet, heat 4 tablespoons oil over low heat. Whisk in the flour and cook, stirring often at first, then almost continuously to prevent sticking and burning, until the roux is very dark brown, 35 to 45 minutes.

Return the browned duck to the stew pot with the onion and pour the roux and 1½ cups stock, broth, or water over the top. Taste and adjust seasonings. Bring to a boil over medium-high heat, then reduce the heat to low, cover tightly, and cook, stirring several times, until the duck is very tender when pierced with a small, sharp knife, about 1½ hours for duck pieces with bones in or about 1 hour for boneless breasts. Stir in a little more stock, broth, or water if the gravy begins to thicken too much; it should remain the consistency of heavy (whipping) cream.

Serve the duck as suggested in the recipe introduction. Sprinkle each portion with green onion and orange zest.
SERVES 6.

Rabbit Stew with Dried Fruit

2 young rabbits with livers (about 5½ to
   6 pounds *total* weight), dressed
1 cup full-bodied red wine such as
   Bordeaux or Zinfandel
¼ cup red wine vinegar
3 garlic cloves, unpeeled
3 or 4 fresh thyme sprigs
4 or 5 fresh parsley sprigs
1 bay leaf
½ teaspoon whole black peppercorns
Salt
3 tablespoons light olive oil
4 tablespoons unsalted butter
6 ounces dried apricots, halved or
   quartered if large, soaked in warm
   water to cover until plump (about 1
   hour)
½ cup golden raisins, soaked in warm
   water to cover until plump (about 1
   hour)
2 tablespoons currant jelly
Honey-glazed dried apricots, halved, for
   garnish (optional)
Flat-leaf parsley leaflets for garnish

This succulent dish, shared by imaginative cook Stephen Suzman, has been known to change the minds of some people who claim not to enjoy eating rabbit.

Quickly rinse the rabbit under cold running water and pat dry with paper toweling. Wrap and refrigerate the livers. Using a small sharp knife, remove the meat from the legs, shoulders, and saddle of the rabbit. Cut the meat into bite-sized pieces.

In a nonreactive container, combine the wine, vinegar, and garlic. Tie the herb sprigs, bay leaf, and peppercorns in a cheesecloth bag and add to the wine mixture. Add the rabbit meat, cover, and refrigerate, stirring several times, for at least 8 hours or for up to 24 hours.

Drain off the rabbit marinade and reserve. Tie the garlic cloves in a cheesecloth bag and reserve along with the herb bag. Pat the meat dry with paper toweling and season to taste with salt.

In a heavy stew pot such as a dutch oven, heat the oil and 2 tablespoons of the butter over medium heat. Add the rabbit and brown on all sides. Reduce the heat to low, add the garlic and seasoning bags, cover, and cook gently for about 20 minutes.

Drain the apricots and raisins and add them and the reserved rabbit marinade to the stew pot. Increase the heat to medium and bring the liquid to a simmer. Reduce the heat to low, cover tightly, and simmer for 10 minutes.

Cut the reserved rabbit liver into bite-sized pieces. Add it to the pot and cook, covered, until the rabbit is tender, about 10 minutes longer.

Using a slotted utensil, remove the rabbit, liver, apricots, and raisins to a bowl. Discard the herb bag. Remove the garlic bag from the stew. Peel the garlic and mash the cloves into a paste. Add it to the simmering liquid along with the remaining 2 tablespoons butter and the jelly and stir until the butter and jelly melt. Return the rabbit, liver, apricots, and raisins to the liquid and heat through.

Garnish each portion with the glazed apricots and herb leaflets.
SERVES 6.

Filipino Chicken and Pork Stew (*Adobo*)

6 chicken thighs
1½ pounds boneless pork, trimmed of
    excess fat
1½ cups cider vinegar
1 cup light soy sauce, or ⅔ cup regular
    soy sauce mixed with
    ⅓ cup water
1 tablespoon coarsely chopped garlic
2 bay leaves
About 2 teaspoons whole black
    peppercorns, lightly crushed
1½ cups homemade chicken stock or
    canned chicken broth, preferably
    low-sodium type
12 ounces fresh mushrooms, preferably
    shiitake, sliced
¼ cup canola oil or other high-quality
    vegetable oil
Minced fresh cilantro (coriander) for
    garnish

The worldwide practice of browning meat before braising it is reversed in this centuries-old method of stewing popular in the Philippines. Cooked white rice is the classic accompaniment to this national dish.

Quickly rinse the chicken and pork and pat dry with paper toweling. Cut the pork into pieces about the same size as the chicken thighs.

In a nonreactive container, combine the chicken, pork, vinegar, soy sauce, garlic, bay leaves, and peppercorns. Marinate at room temperature for 1 hour; turn the meats 2 or 3 times.

Transfer the meats and marinade to a large, heavy saucepan or stew pot. Add the stock or broth and bring almost to a boil over medium-high heat. Reduce the heat to low, cover, and simmer until the chicken is tender when pierced with the tines of a fork or a wooden skewer, about 35 minutes. Using a slotted utensil or tongs, remove the chicken to a platter. Cover and simmer until the pork is tender, about 40 minutes longer. Remove the pork to the platter with the chicken.

Increase the heat and bring the liquid to a boil. Add the mushrooms and cook until the liquid is reduced to about 1½ cups, about 15 minutes. Remove the pan from the heat, discard the bay leaves, and let the liquid stand until cooled to room temperature. Skim off any fat that rises to the surface.

In a large sauté pan or skillet, heat the oil over high heat. Add the chicken and pork pieces, a few at a time, and brown on all sides. Transfer the browned meat to a platter and keep warm while browning the rest of the meat. Quickly reheat the sauce and pour it over the chicken and pork.

Sprinkle each portion with cilantro.

SERVES 6.

New Mexican Green Chile Pork Stew

1 pound tomatillos (green husk
    tomatoes), papery husks removed
4 tablespoons high-quality vegetable oil
2 cups finely chopped yellow onion
6 fresh large green mild chiles such as
    Anaheim, stemmed, seeded (if desired),
    and finely chopped (about 2 pounds)
2 fresh green hot chiles such as serrano or
    jalapeño, stemmed, seeded (if desired),
    and finely chopped
1 tablespoon minced or pressed garlic
¼ cup chopped fresh cilantro (coriander)
2 cups homemade pork or chicken stock
    or canned chicken broth, preferably
    low-sodium type
3 pounds boneless pork, trimmed of
    excess fat and cut into 1-inch cubes
2 teaspoons minced fresh oregano, or
    1 teaspoon crumbled dried oregano
All-purpose flour for dredging
Finely diced fresh red and green sweet
    peppers and/or hot chiles for garnish

In New Mexico, this traditional stew is usually prepared with fiery hot green chiles. Since most of us only have access to less explosive varieties such as Anaheim, I've used a combination of mild and hot chiles. Vary the amount of hot chiles according to preference; leaving the seeds in adds more intensity.

Place the tomatillos in a saucepan and add water to cover. Bring to a boil over medium-high heat. Cook for 5 minutes. Drain, rinse, and drain again. Set aside.

In a sauté pan or heavy skillet, heat 2 tablespoons of the oil over medium heat. Add the onion and chopped mild and hot chiles and sauté until soft, about 10 minutes. Add the garlic and sauté for 1 minute longer. Stir in the cilantro and stock or broth. Bring to a boil and cook for about 4 minutes.

Transfer the onion-chile mixture to a food processor or blender and chop finely. Add the reserved tomatillos and purée until fairly smooth.

Quickly rinse the pork under running cold water and pat dry with paper toweling. Sprinkle the pork with about half of the oregano. Dredge the pork in flour to coat lightly all over. Shake off excess flour.

In a heavy stew pot such as a dutch oven, heat the remaining 2 tablespoons oil over medium-high heat. Add as many of the pork cubes as will fit comfortably without overcrowding the pot and brown on all sides. Using a slotted utensil or tongs, transfer the browned pork to a plate. Brown the remaining pork cubes in the same manner, adding more oil as necessary to prevent sticking.

When all the meat is browned, return it to the pan. Pour the tomatillo mixture over the pork and scrape up any browned bits from the bottom of the pan. Bring to a boil over high heat, then reduce the heat to low, cover, and simmer until the pork is very tender when pierced with a meat fork or small, sharp knife, 45 minutes to 1 hour. Add a bit of stock or broth if the stew begins to dry out.

Sprinkle each portion with the diced sweet peppers and/or chiles.
SERVES 6.

Peruvian Spicy Pork Stew

¾ pound ground pork with some fat
½ pound ground lean beef
2 teaspoons minced or pressed garlic
¼ cup chile powder, preferably from
    ancho or pasilla chiles, or to taste
1 teaspoon ground cinnamon
¾ teaspoon ground cumin
⅛ teaspoon ground cloves
About 1½ cups water
4 tablespoons vegetable oil
2 pounds boneless lean pork, cut into
    1-inch cubes
2 cups finely chopped yellow onion
3 fresh green or red jalapeño or other hot
    chiles, stemmed, seeded, deveined, and
    finely chopped
About ¾ cup homemade chicken stock or
    canned chicken broth, preferably
    low-sodium type
1¼ cups tomato juice
About 1 teaspoon salt
About ¼ teaspoon ground cayenne
About ¼ teaspoon freshly ground black
    pepper
Minced fresh cilantro for garnish

I've shown this fiery dish accompanied by Ellen's Carrot Cake (page 93), but it is also great with Mashed Potatoes (page 89). Or try serving it with mashed yam varieties of sweet potatoes to counteract the heat.

In a heavy stew pot such as a dutch oven, combine the ground meats over medium heat. Breaking up the meats with a wooden spoon and moving them continuously, cook until the meats just begin to lose their pink color; do not brown. Stir in 1 teaspoon of the garlic, the chile powder, cinnamon, cumin, and cloves. Add ¾ cup of the water. Reduce the heat to low and simmer, uncovered, for about 1 hour, adding additional water a little at a time as needed to keep the mixture from drying out. Near the end of the cooking, allow the water to evaporate.

Meanwhile, quickly rinse the pork under running cold water and pat dry with paper toweling.

In a sauté pan or skillet over medium-high heat, heat the oil. Add as many of the pork cubes as will fit comfortably without crowding the pot and brown on all sides. Using a slotted utensil or tongs, transfer the browned pork to a plate. Brown the remaining pork cubes in the same manner, adding more oil as necessary to prevent sticking.

Add the onion and chiles to the ground meat mixture. Increase the heat to medium-high and sauté until the onion is soft, about 5 minutes. Add the remaining 1 teaspoon garlic and sauté for 1 minute longer. Add the browned pork and stir well. Add ¾ cup stock or broth and the tomato juice and bring almost to a boil. Reduce the heat to low, cover, and simmer until the meat is tender, about 1 hour. While cooking, season to taste with salt and black and cayenne peppers. Add more stock or broth if the stew becomes too dry.

Sprinkle each portion with the cilantro.
SERVES 6.

Moroccan Lamb *Tagine*

1 teaspoon coriander seed
1 cinnamon stick (4 inches), broken into
    several pieces, or 1 tablespoon ground
    cinnamon
¼ cup sesame seed
3 pounds boneless lamb leg or shoulder,
    cut into 1½-inch cubes
About 3 cups homemade lamb or
    vegetable stock, reconstituted
    vegetable bouillon, or water
2 cups finely chopped yellow onion
1 teaspoon minced or pressed garlic
¼ cup fresh or canned tomato purée
3 tablespoons fruity olive oil, preferably
    extra-virgin
1 tablespoon minced fresh rosemary, or
    1 teaspoon crumbled dried rosemary
½ teaspoon crumbled saffron threads, or
    ¼ teaspoon ground saffron
About 1 teaspoon salt
About 1 teaspoon freshly ground black
    pepper
12 ounces pitted prunes
3 tablespoons honey, or to taste
Orange flower water (available where
    alcoholic drink mixes are sold)

During the days when Lin Cotton and I ran a catering company, we once served this Moroccan stew to 100 costumed guests seated at low tables on rose-petal-sprinkled Persian carpets and pillows in a tent draped with gauze hangings and exotic lamps. Later I served it in a dense redwood grove to 40 guests on Lin's fortieth birthday.

Unlike most other stews, the meat is not browned when making a *tagine*. Couscous or brown rice is a good accompaniment. For each serving, place a scoopful alongside the *tagine* in a shallow bowl or deep plate.

In a small, heavy skillet, heat the coriander seed over medium heat, stirring or shaking the pan quite frequently, until fragrant, about 3 minutes. Be careful not to burn the seed. Pour the seed onto a plate to cool, then transfer to an electric spice grinder. If using stick cinnamon, add the pieces to the seed and grind until pulverized. Set aside. If using ground cinnamon, stir it into the coriander seed and set aside.

In a small, heavy skillet, heat the sesame seed over medium heat, stirring or shaking the pan quite frequently, until lightly toasted, about 5 minutes. Be careful not to burn the seed. Pour onto a plate to cool.

Quickly rinse the lamb under cold running water and place it in a heavy stew pot such as a dutch oven. Add enough stock, bouillon, or water to cover barely. Add the onion, garlic, tomato purée, oil, rosemary, coriander-cinnamon mixture, saffron, and salt and pepper to taste. Bring to a boil over medium-high heat, then reduce the heat to low, cover, and simmer until the meat is tender, about 2 hours. Add a little more liquid if the stew becomes too dry.

Meanwhile, cover the prunes with warm water and soak until plumped, about 1 hour. Drain the prunes, stir them into the stew, and cook for about 15 minutes. Stir in the honey and simmer for about 10 minutes longer.

Sprinkle each portion with orange flower water and the toasted sesame seeds.
SERVES 6.

Turkish Lamb and Okra Stew

3 pounds boneless lamb, trimmed of
    excess fat and cut into 1-inch cubes
About ½ cup fruity olive oil, preferably
    extra-virgin
1 teaspoon minced or pressed garlic
4 teaspoons minced fresh rosemary, or
    2 teaspoons crumbled dried rosemary
1 tablespoon ground cinnamon
1½ teaspoons ground coriander
Salt
Freshly ground black pepper
¼ cup (½ stick) unsalted butter
3 cups finely chopped yellow onion
About 2 cups homemade lamb or chicken
    stock or canned chicken broth,
    preferably low-sodium type
3 cups peeled, seeded, and chopped fresh
    or drained canned plum tomatoes
    (about 1½ pounds)
2 tablespoons tomato paste
2½ pounds small okra
4 tablespoons freshly squeezed lemon juice
Minced fresh parsley, preferably flat-leaf
    type, for garnish

If you wish to crown this succulent stew with crispy Phyllo Crowns (page 93), prepare the phyllo toppings while the lamb is cooking. Refrigerate them until the stew comes out of the oven, and then bake them. Crown each portion just before serving to prevent the crisp pastry from becoming soggy.

Quickly rinse the lamb under running cold water and shake off excess water.

In a nonreactive bowl, combine ¼ cup of the oil, garlic, rosemary, cinnamon, coriander, and salt and pepper to taste. Add the lamb and stir to coat the meat well. Set aside for about 1 hour, stirring occasionally.

Remove the lamb from the marinade and pat dry with paper toweling.

In a heavy stew pot such as a dutch oven, combine the remaining ¼ cup oil and the butter over medium-high heat. When the butter melts, add as many of the lamb cubes as will fit comfortably without crowding the pot and brown on all sides. Using a slotted utensil or tongs, transfer the lamb to a plate. Brown the remaining lamb cubes in the same manner, adding more oil as necessary to prevent sticking.

Preheat an oven to 325° F.

Add the onion to the same pot in which the lamb was browned and sauté until soft, about 5 minutes. Stir in the stock or broth and scrape up any brown bits from the pan. Return the meat to the pot, lower the heat, and simmer until the broth has almost evaporated, about 10 minutes.

Stir the tomatoes and tomato paste into the stew and season to taste with salt and pepper. Cover the pot and transfer it to the oven. Cook, stirring occasionally, until the lamb is very tender when pierced with a small, sharp knife or a wooden skewer, 1½ to 2 hours. Add a little more stock or broth if the stew becomes too dry.

Meanwhile, carefully cut off and discard the stem ends from the okra; avoid cutting into the pods.

About 20 minutes before the stew is done, bring a pot of water to a boil over medium-high heat. Add the okra pods and 2 tablespoons of the lemon juice and cook for 5 minutes. Drain the okra pods well, then stir them into the stew and simmer until the meat is tender. Just before serving, stir in the remaining 2 tablespoons lemon juice.

Sprinkle each portion with parsley.

SERVES 6.

Lamb Stew with Caramelized Vegetables

3 pounds lean lamb from leg or shoulder, trimmed of excess fat and cut into 1½-inch cubes
About 8 tablespoons fruity olive oil, preferably extra-virgin
2 cups chopped yellow onion
1 tablespoon minced or pressed garlic
⅓ cup hearty red wine such as California Zinfandel or Italian Barolo
⅓ cup red wine vinegar
3 cups peeled, seeded, and finely chopped or coarsely puréed fresh or canned plum tomatoes with their juice (about 1½ pounds)
¼ cup chopped fresh chervil or parsley, preferably flat-leaf type
2 tablespoons minced fresh rosemary or thyme, or 2 teaspoons crumbled dried rosemary or thyme
Salt
Freshly ground black pepper
Caramelized Vegetables (page 90)
Chopped fresh chervil or parsley for garnish
Fresh rosemary or thyme sprigs for garnish

This meltingly tender winter stew should be served over the soft variation (polentina) of Basic Polenta (page 88), although it is also good with rice or other cooked grains. Prepare the polenta about 45 minutes before the stew is done and keep it warm.

Quickly rinse the lamb under running cold water and pat dry with paper toweling.

In a heavy stew pot such as a dutch oven, heat 4 tablespoons of the oil over high heat. Add as many of the lamb cubes as will fit comfortably without crowding the pot and brown on all sides. Using a slotted utensil or tongs, transfer the lamb to a plate. Brown the remaining lamb cubes in the same manner, adding more oil as necessary to prevent sticking.

To the same pot used for browning the lamb, add 2 tablespoons of the oil and warm over medium heat. Add the onion and sauté until golden, about 10 minutes. Add the garlic and sauté for 1 minute longer. Add the wine and vinegar and cook for about 2 minutes, scraping the pan bottom to loosen any browned bits.

Return the browned lamb to the pot and add the tomatoes, chervil or parsley, rosemary or thyme, and salt and pepper to taste; stir well. Increase the heat to high and bring to a boil. Cover, reduce the heat to very low, and simmer until the meat is very tender when pierced with a small, sharp knife or a wooden skewer, about 1½ to 2 hours. Add a little water if the stew dries out before the meat is tender.

Alternatively, transfer the covered stew to a preheated 350° F oven and cook, stirring occasionally, until the meat is tender, 1½ to 2 hours.

About 45 minutes before the stew is done, prepare the Caramelized Vegetables and keep them warm.

A few minutes before serving, stir the vegetables into the stew.

Garnish each portion with the minced chervil or parsley and the herb sprigs.

SERVES 6.

White Veal Stew *(Blanquette de Veau)*

3 pounds boneless veal, trimmed of excess
    fat and cut into 1-inch cubes
About 12 tablespoons (1½ sticks) unsalted
    butter
1 cup finely chopped leek, white and pale
    green portions only
1 cup finely chopped white or yellow
    onion
1 cup finely chopped celery
1 teaspoon minced or pressed garlic
1 bay leaf, crumbled
2 tablespoons minced fresh chervil, dill,
    or parsley, preferably flat-leaf type
1 teaspoon minced or grated fresh lemon
    zest
About 3 cups homemade veal or chicken
    stock, or 3 cups canned chicken broth,
    preferably low-sodium type
Salt
Freshly ground white pepper
1 pound pearl onions
8 ounces fresh small white button
    mushrooms
2 tablespoons all-purpose flour
1 cup heavy (whipping) cream
2 cups shelled fresh or thawed frozen
    green peas (about 2 pounds)
8 ounces tender asparagus, trimmed and
    cut on the diagonal into 1-inch lengths
¼ cup freshly squeezed lemon juice
Fresh chervil, dill, or parsley sprigs,
    preferably flat-leaf type, for garnish

This delicately seasoned stew, prepared throughout France by both chefs and home cooks, celebrates the arrival of spring. Avoid using a cast-iron pot, which can darken the light color of the stew.

Quickly rinse the veal under running cold water and pat dry with paper toweling.

In a heavy stew pot, melt 6 tablespoons of the butter over medium heat. Add as many of the veal cubes as will fit comfortably without crowding the pot and sear lightly on all sides; do not brown. With a slotted utensil or tongs, transfer the veal to a plate. Sear the remaining veal cubes in the same manner, adding more butter as necessary to prevent sticking.

To the same pot used for searing the veal, add 4 tablespoons of the butter and melt over medium heat. Add the leek, onion, and celery and sauté until the vegetables are soft but not browned, about 8 minutes. Add the garlic, bay leaf, minced herb, and lemon zest and sauté for 1 minute. Return the veal to the pot. Pour in enough stock or broth to cover barely and season to taste with salt and pepper. Bring to a boil, then cover partially, reduce the heat to low, and simmer for 30 minutes.

Add the pearl onions and mushrooms to the stew and continue simmering, stirring occasionally, until the vegetables and veal are tender, 45 minutes to 1 hour. Add a little more stock or broth if the stew becomes too dry.

Strain the liquid from the stew into a vessel with a pouring spout and set the stew aside. In a heavy saucepan, melt the remaining 2 tablespoons butter over medium-low heat. Stir in the flour and cook, stirring, for 3 to 4 minutes; do not brown. Gradually whisk in the reserved cooking liquid, then stir in the cream and bring to a boil. Reduce the heat to medium and simmer until reduced to about 3 cups, about 15 minutes.

Meanwhile, steam or boil the peas and asparagus separately until tender-crisp. Plunge into cold water to halt cooking and preserve color. Drain well.

Stir the lemon juice into the reduced cream sauce and season to taste with salt and pepper. Stir in the reserved veal-vegetable mixture, the drained peas and asparagus, and the minced herb. Taste and adjust seasonings. Gently heat the stew to serving temperature, about 3 minutes.

Garnish each portion with the herb sprigs.

SERVES 6.

Italian Veal Stew

3 pounds boneless veal, trimmed of excess
    fat and cut into 1-inch cubes
All-purpose flour for dredging
About 3 tablespoons olive oil
About 3 tablespoons unsalted butter
3 tablespoons finely chopped shallot
1¼ cups dry white wine
2 tablespoons minced fresh sage leaves, or
    2 teaspoons crumbled dried sage
About 1 teaspoon salt
About 1 teaspoon freshly ground white
    pepper
Puff Pastry Cutouts (page 93) for garnish
    (optional)
Fresh marjoram, oregano, or savory
    sprigs for garnish

To add a bit of piquancy to this classic dish, stir in 2 to 3 tablespoons well-drained capers or chopped pitted olives a few minutes before serving.

Quickly rinse the veal under cold running water and pat dry with paper toweling. Dredge the meat in flour to coat lightly all over. Shake off excess flour.

In a sauté pan or heavy stew pot such as a dutch oven, combine 3 tablespoons oil and 3 tablespoons butter over medium-high heat. When the butter melts, add as many of the veal cubes as will fit comfortably without crowding the pot and brown well on all sides. Using a slotted utensil or tongs, transfer the veal to a plate. Brown the remaining veal cubes in the same manner, adding more oil and butter as necessary to prevent sticking.

To the same pot used for browning the veal, add the shallot and sauté until soft, about 3 minutes. Pour the wine into the pan, increase the heat to high, and scrape the pan bottom to loosen any browned bits. Reduce the heat to low and return the veal to the pan. Stir in the sage and season to taste with salt and pepper. Cover and simmer, turning the meat occasionally, until the veal tests tender when pierced with a small, sharp knife or a wooden skewer, about 1 hour.

Meanwhile, prepare the puff pastry (if used).

Arrange several pieces of puff pastry on top of each portion and garnish with the herb sprigs.

SERVES 6.

Braised Veal Shanks *(Ossobuco)*

8 large veal shanks (about 14 ounces *each*)
Salt
Freshly ground black pepper
All-purpose flour for dredging
About 2 tablespoons unsalted butter
About 2 tablespoons fruity olive oil,
    preferably extra-virgin
1 cup finely chopped yellow onion
½ cup finely chopped carrot
½ cup finely chopped celery
1 teaspoon minced or pressed garlic
½ teaspoon minced fresh sage, or
    ¼ teaspoon crumbled dried sage
½ teaspoon minced fresh rosemary, or
    ¼ teaspoon crumbled dried rosemary
1 bay leaf, crumbled
1 cup dry white wine
3 tablespoons fresh or canned tomato
    purée
2 cups homemade veal, beef, or chicken
    stock or canned beef or chicken broth,
    preferably low-sodium type
About 1 tablespoon soy sauce, preferably
    tamari

GREMOLADA
3 tablespoons minced fresh parsley
1 teaspoon minced or pressed garlic
1 tablespoon minced or grated fresh
    lemon zest

Fresh parsley sprigs, preferably flat-leaf
    type, for garnish

A number of years ago, Luciano Parolari, chef at Lake Como's world-class Villa d'Este Hotel, showed me how to prepare this Lombardian specialty. On one occasion when the meat did not look as brown as I thought it should, I discovered the additional color and flavor contributed by soy sauce.

You'll want to provide small spoons or forks for diners to dig out the marvelously flavored soft marrow from the bone.

Although saffron-infused *risotto alla milanese* traditionally accompanies *ossobuco,* I've shown it here with a risotto laced with wild mushrooms. For a basic risotto recipe, see my *Rice Cookbook.*

Quickly rinse the veal shanks under running cold water and pat dry with paper toweling. Lightly salt and pepper the veal shanks. Dredge the meat in flour to coat lightly all over. Shake off the excess flour.

In a heavy sauté pan or stew pot such as a dutch oven, combine the butter and oil over medium-high heat. When the butter melts, add a few of the veal shanks, being careful not to crowd the pan, and brown well on all sides. Using tongs, remove the shanks to a plate. Brown the remaining shanks in the same manner, adding butter and oil as necessary to prevent sticking.

To the same pot used for browning the shanks, add the onion, carrot, and celery and sauté over medium heat until soft but not browned, about 5 minutes. Stir in the garlic, sage, rosemary, and bay leaf and sauté for 1 minute longer. Add the wine, increase the heat to medium-high, bring to a boil, and cook until most of the liquid evaporates, about 5 minutes.

Arrange the browned meat in the pan with the vegetables, keeping the shanks upright to prevent the marrow from escaping. Add the tomato purée, stock or broth, and soy sauce to taste. Bring to a boil, then cover, reduce the heat to low, and simmer until the meat is tender, about 1½ hours.

To make the *gremolada,* combine all the ingredients in a small bowl. Sprinkle the mixture evenly over the tops of the shanks about 5 minutes before serving.

Garnish each portion with parsley sprigs.

SERVES 8.

Red Wine Beef

8 ounces slab bacon, preferably
  pepper-cured type, cut into small dice
3 pounds beef round or other boneless
  lean beef, trimmed of excess fat and
  cut into 1-inch cubes
1½ cups chopped red onion
1 teaspoon minced or pressed garlic
Salt
Freshly ground black pepper
3 tablespoons all-purpose flour
About 2 cups full-bodied red wine such as
  French Burgundy, Italian Barolo, or
  California Pinot Noir
About 2 cups homemade beef stock or
  canned beef broth, preferably
  low-sodium type
3 tablespoons fresh or canned tomato
  purée
3 tablespoons minced fresh parsley
1 tablespoon minced fresh thyme, or
  1 teaspoon crumbled dried thyme
1 bay leaf
1 pound pearl onions, unpeeled
3 tablespoons unsalted butter
8 ounces fresh mushrooms, preferably
  wild varieties, sliced
3 tablespoons minced fresh parsley,
  preferably flat-leaf type
Whole fresh chives, preferably with
  flowers, for garnish

Based on classic *boeuf à la bourguignonne*, this hearty yet simple stew may be made with any full-bodied red wine. It's not a time to skimp on the quality of the wine, since all of the flavor remains.

In a heavy stew pot such as a dutch oven, cook the bacon over medium-high heat until crisp. Using a slotted utensil, remove the bacon to paper toweling to drain. Pour off and reserve the fat rendered from the bacon. Return 1 tablespoon of the bacon drippings to the pot and place over medium heat. Add as many of the beef cubes as will fit comfortably without crowding the pot and brown lightly on all sides. Using a slotted utensil or tongs, transfer the beef to a plate. Brown the remaining beef cubes in the same manner, adding bacon drippings as necessary to prevent sticking.

Preheat an oven to 350° F.

To the same pot used for browning the beef, add 1 tablespoon of the reserved bacon drippings. Add the chopped onion and sauté over medium-high heat until the onion is soft, about 5 minutes. Add the garlic and sauté for 1 minute longer.

Season the beef to taste with salt and pepper and sprinkle it with the flour. Add the meat to the onion and sauté until the flour is lightly browned, about 3 minutes.

Pour in the wine and enough stock or broth to cover barely. Stir in the tomato purée and herbs. Bring to a boil, then cover the pot and transfer it to the oven. Cook until the beef is tender, about 2 hours. Add a little more wine and/or stock if the stew becomes too dry.

Meanwhile, cut a small *X* in the root end of each pearl onion. Drop the onions into a pot of boiling water. Return to a boil and cook for 5 minutes. Drain the onions, rinse under cold running water, and drain again. As soon as the onions are cool enough to handle, peel and reserve them.

In a sauté pan or heavy skillet, melt the butter over medium-high heat. Add the mushrooms and sauté for about 2 minutes. Reduce the heat to medium-low and cook until tender, about 8 minutes longer. Set aside.

When the stew is tender, stir in the reserved bacon, pearl onions, and mushrooms and heat through. Taste and adjust the seasonings.

Sprinkle each portion with the minced parsley and garnish with the chives.
SERVES 6.

Beijing Star Anise Beef

3 pounds beef round or other boneless
  lean beef, trimmed of excess fat and
  cut into 1-inch cubes
Salt
Freshly ground black pepper
About 4 tablespoons high-quality
  vegetable oil
1 cup chopped yellow onion
½ cup sliced green onion
2 tablespoons minced fresh ginger root
1 teaspoon minced or pressed garlic
6 tablespoons soy sauce, preferably tamari
6 tablespoons Chinese rice wine
  (Shaoxing) or dry sherry
3 tablespoons rice wine vinegar
3 tablespoons light brown sugar
3 star anise
8 ounces fresh shiitake mushrooms, sliced
2 tablespoons cornstarch
6 tablespoons water
Stir-fried snow peas, cut into julienne, for
  garnish
Sliced kumquats for garnish (optional)

Eight-pointed star anise are pods that hold tiny seeds and impart an exotic flavor; they're available in Asian markets and many supermarkets alongside other spices. If fresh shiitake mushrooms are unavailable, soak about 8 dried black mushrooms in warm water to cover until soft, about 30 minutes; drain, discard tough stems, and slice.

Serve with fluffy white rice.

Quickly rinse the beef under cold running water and pat dry with paper toweling. Sprinkle lightly with salt and pepper and set aside.

In a heavy stew pot such as a dutch oven, heat 3 tablespoons of the oil over medium heat. Add as many of the beef pieces as will fit comfortably without crowding and brown on all sides. Using a slotted utensil or tongs, transfer the beef to a plate. Brown the remaining beef cubes in the same manner, adding more oil as necessary to prevent sticking.

To the same pot used to brown the beef, add enough oil to that remaining in the pot to equal 2 tablespoons. Add the yellow onion and sauté until soft, about 3 minutes. Add the green onion, ginger, and garlic and sauté for 1 minute longer. Return the beef to the pan. Add the soy sauce, rice wine or sherry, vinegar, brown sugar, and star anise. Season generously to taste with pepper. Bring to a boil over medium-high heat, then cover tightly, reduce the heat to low, and simmer until the meat is very tender, 2 to 2½ hours. About 30 minutes before the meat is tender, stir in the mushrooms.

Using a slotted utensil, transfer the beef and mushrooms to a bowl. Strain the cooking liquid into a saucepan or flameproof casserole. Remove excess fat from the top of the liquid. Combine the cornstarch and water in a small bowl, then stir the mixture into the stew liquid. Place over medium heat and cook until thickened to a sauce consistency, about 5 minutes. Return the beef and mushrooms to the pot and simmer until heated through.

Serve with rice and sprinkle each portion with the snow peas and kumquats (if used).

SERVES 6.

Hungarian Goulash and Dumplings

3 pounds beef round or other boneless
    lean beef, trimmed of excess fat and
    cut into 1-inch cubes
Salt
Freshly ground black pepper
About 4 tablespoons fruity olive oil,
    preferably extra-virgin
1½ cups chopped yellow onion
1 cup diced or chopped red sweet pepper
1 tablespoon minced or pressed garlic
1½ tablespoons sweet paprika, preferably
    Hungarian
1 teaspoon caraway seed
2 cups homemade beef stock or canned
    beef broth, preferably low-sodium type
1 cup dry white wine
⅓ cup fresh or canned tomato purée
2 teaspoons minced fresh tarragon or
    oregano, or ½ teaspoon dried tarragon
    or oregano

HUNGARIAN DUMPLINGS
(CSIPETKE)
2 cups all-purpose flour
½ teaspoon salt
2 eggs
3 cups homemade beef stock or canned
    beef broth
¼ cup (½ stick) unsalted butter, melted
1 tablespoon caraway seed

Fresh tarragon or oregano sprigs for
    garnish

This ancient dish originated from the practice of nomadic shepherds, known as *gulyás,* adding whatever meat could be killed each day to a communal cauldron simmering over a campfire. You may omit the dumplings and serve the stew over flat egg noodles tossed in melted butter and caraway seed. Add a dollop of sour cream or crème fraîche to each serving if you enjoy extra richness.

Quickly rinse the beef under cold running water and pat dry with paper toweling. Season to taste with salt and pepper.

In a heavy stew pot such as a dutch oven, heat 3 tablespoons of the oil over medium-high heat. Add as many of the beef cubes as will fit comfortably without crowding and brown lightly on all sides. Using a slotted utensil or tongs, transfer the beef to a plate. Brown the remaining beef cubes in the same manner, adding more oil as necessary to prevent sticking.

To the same pot in which the meat was browned, add enough oil to that remaining in the pot to equal 2 tablespoons. When the oil is hot, add the onion and sweet pepper and sauté until the vegetables are soft but not browned, about 5 minutes. Add the garlic, paprika, and caraway seed and sauté for 1 minute longer. Add the stock or broth, wine, tomato purée, and minced or dried tarragon or oregano and bring to a boil over medium-high heat. Reduce the heat to low, cover tightly, and simmer until the meat is tender, 1½ to 2 hours.

Meanwhile, to make the dumplings, combine the flour and salt in a bowl. Make a well in the center, add the eggs, and, using a fork, gradually mix the flour into the eggs to form a stiff dough. Transfer the dough to a lightly floured work surface and knead vigorously, adding a few drops of water as necessary, until the dough is smooth and pliable.

To cook the dumplings, pour the stock or broth into a saucepan and bring to a simmer over medium heat. Pull off pieces of the dough a little smaller than a walnut and roll the dough into balls between your palms. Drop some of the dough balls into the simmering broth, being careful not to crowd the pan. Cook the balls until they float to the top and are done all the way through, about 5 minutes. At the same time, combine the butter and caraway seed in a medium saucepan over very low heat. Using a slotted utensil, transfer the cooked dumplings to the melted butter and toss well. Cook the remaining dough balls in the same manner; keep warm.

Serve the goulash with the dumplings. Garnish each portion with herb sprigs.
SERVES 6.

Venison Stew

1 cup Madeira wine
1 cup full-bodied red wine
¼ cup red wine vinegar
½ cup light olive oil
1 tablespoon minced or pressed garlic
2 tablespoons minced fresh thyme, or
  2 teaspoons crumbled dried thyme
1 tablespoon juniper berries, lightly
  crushed
2 fresh bay leaves, minced, or 1 dried bay
  leaf, crumbled
About 2 teaspoons freshly ground black
  pepper
3 pounds boneless venison, cut into
  1-inch cubes
Salt
8 ounces thickly sliced bacon, chopped
About 2 tablespoons high-quality
  vegetable oil (if needed)
2 cups chopped yellow onion
3 tablespoons all-purpose flour
About 1 cup homemade beef stock or
  canned beef broth, preferably
  low-sodium type
3 pounds baby turnips, peeled, or larger
  turnips, peeled and cut into bite-sized
  pieces
1 cup dried cranberries, soaked in water
  to cover for about 1 hour
3 tablespoons minced fresh orange zest
3 tablespoons minced fresh thyme or
  parsley, preferably flat-leaf type, for
  garnish
Fresh thyme or parsley sprigs for garnish

When made with tenderloins of venison, now available at many better meat markets, this stew is meltingly succulent. But any venison cut will be delicious, although other cuts will need longer cooking. Venison is also available by mail order; check gourmet magazine ads for current sources.

In a large nonreactive bowl, combine the Madeira, red wine, vinegar, olive oil, garlic, 2 tablespoons minced thyme, juniper berries, bay leaves, and pepper to taste.

Quickly rinse the meat under cold running water and shake off excess water. Sprinkle the meat lightly with salt and add it to the marinade, stir well, cover, and let stand at room temperature for 2 hours, or refrigerate for up to 24 hours, stirring occasionally.

Preheat an oven to 350° F. Drain the venison, reserving the marinade, and pat the meat dry with paper toweling. Strain the marinade and set aside.

In a heavy stew pot such as a dutch oven, cook the bacon over medium heat until the fat is rendered. Using a slotted utensil, remove the bacon to a plate and set aside. Add as many of the venison cubes as will fit comfortably without crowding the pot and brown lightly on all sides. Using a slotted utensil or tongs, transfer the venison to a plate. Brown the remaining venison cubes in the same manner, adding more vegetable oil as necessary to prevent sticking.

To the same pot in which the meat was browned, add enough vegetable oil to the fat remaining in the pot to equal about 2 tablespoons. Add the onion and sauté until soft and golden, about 10 minutes.

Sprinkle the meat with the flour and stir to mix well. Return the meat to the pot with the onion and sauté for about 2 minutes. Stir in the strained marinade and the stock or broth. Bring to a boil over medium-high heat, then cover tightly and transfer the pot to the oven. Cook for about 20 minutes, then stir in the turnips and continue to cook until the venison is very tender, about 45 minutes to 1 hour longer.

About 20 minutes before the venison is done, drain the cranberries and stir them into the stew, along with about 1½ tablespoons of the orange zest.

Sprinkle each portion with the remaining orange zest and minced thyme or parsley and garnish with the herb sprigs.
SERVES 6.

CASSEROLES

Breakfast Dairy Casserole

12 to 16 homemade or frozen cheese
   blintzes, each about 4 inches long and
   1 inch wide
½ cup (1 stick) unsalted butter
6 eggs
2 cups sour cream
¼ cup sugar
¼ cup freshly squeezed orange juice
2 tablespoons freshly squeezed lemon juice
2 teaspoons vanilla extract
About ¼ teaspoon salt
2 tablespoons sugar mixed with
   1 tablespoon ground cinnamon
Finely julienned fresh orange zest for
   garnish
3 to 4 cups fresh berries such as
   blueberries, strawberries, raspberries,
   blackberries, or currants (one type or
   a mixture)

**Shirley Berger, my assistant Ellen's mom, originated this recipe that can
start with cheese blintzes made from scratch, using a favorite recipe.
Using purchased frozen ones is certainly easier and the end result tastes
great.**

Prepare the blintzes or slightly thaw frozen blintzes.

Preheat an oven to 350° F. Place ¼ cup of the butter in a 9-by-13-inch baking
dish and set it in the warming oven until melted.

In a sauté pan or skillet, melt the remaining ¼ cup butter over medium-high
heat. Add the blintzes, a few at a time so as not to crowd the pan, and lightly
brown them on each side. Transfer the browned blintzes to a plate. Brown the
remaining blintzes in the same manner. Arrange the blintzes in a single layer in
the baking dish containing the melted butter.

In a mixing bowl, beat the eggs well. Add the sour cream, sugar, orange and
lemon juices, vanilla, and salt to taste. Whisk until smooth. Pour the mixture
over the blintzes. Sprinkle with the cinnamon-sugar mixture and bake until the
custard is set, about 45 minutes.

To serve, cut into squares, allowing 2 blintzes per serving. Sprinkle each
portion with orange zest and berries.

SERVES 6 TO 8.

Southwestern Tamale Casserole

Black Beans (page 91)
1 cup milk
2 cups freshly cut, thawed frozen, or drained canned corn kernels (from about 4 medium-sized ears)
2 cups Mexican corn flour (*masa harina*)
1½ cups (3 sticks) unsalted butter, at room temperature
2 teaspoons baking powder
Salt
2 tablespoons high-quality vegetable oil
1½ cups chopped yellow onion
3 fresh green mild chiles such as poblano, stemmed and finely chopped
2 teaspoons minced or pressed garlic
1 teaspoon ground cumin
About 1 teaspoon chile powder, preferably from ancho or pasilla chiles
¼ cup chopped fresh mint
8 ounces very fresh goat's milk cheese, crumbled
8 ounces Monterey Jack or cheddar cheese, freshly shredded
Shredded fresh mint for garnish

Mexican corn flour (*masa harina*) is finely ground dehydrated dough used for making tamales. Although it may be difficult to locate outside of the Southwest, blue corn flour makes a very tasty version of this dish. But the dish also works well with the more readily available yellow variety.

Instead of the black bean mixture, the casserole may be filled with crumbled cooked chorizo or a favorite meat or bean chili.

Prepare the black beans. Drain and set aside.

In a saucepan over medium heat, combine the milk and corn. Bring to a boil, then reduce the heat to low and simmer until the corn is tender, 10 to 12 minutes. Pour the mixture into a food processor and purée coarsely. Transfer to a bowl and stir in the corn flour.

In a large bowl, combine the butter, baking powder, and 1 teaspoon salt and beat until soft and fluffy. Add the corn flour mixture, a little at a time, and beat until the mixture is light and fluffy. Set aside.

Preheat an oven to 350° F.

In a sauté pan or skillet over medium-high heat, heat the vegetable oil. Add the onion and green chile and sauté until the onion is soft and golden, about 5 minutes. Add the garlic, cumin, and chile powder to taste and sauté for 1 minute longer. Remove from the heat and stir in the drained beans and chopped mint. Season to taste with salt and mix well.

Grease a 9-by-13-inch baking dish and press half of the corn flour mixture in an even layer in the dish. Distribute the bean mixture evenly over the corn mixture. Top with half of each of the cheeses, then cover with the remaining corn mixture. Sprinkle all of the remaining cheese over the top. Bake until the cheese melts and the casserole is heated through, about 30 minutes.

To serve, cut into squares and sprinkle each portion with shredded mint.

SERVES 6 AS A MAIN COURSE, OR 8 TO 10 AS SIDE DISH.

Chicken Parmigiana

5 boned and skinned chicken breast halves
3 eggs
2 cups crushed corn flakes or fresh bread
    crumbs
About ½ cup (1 stick) unsalted butter or
    light olive oil, or ¼ cup *each* butter
    and olive oil
1 pound fresh mushrooms, sliced
1½ cups pitted ripe olives, sliced
2 pounds very small artichokes
    (1½ to 2 ounces *each*), trimmed and
    thinly sliced lengthwise, or 8½ ounces
    canned artichokes (not marinated),
    drained and thinly sliced lengthwise
1½ cups (about 6 ounces) freshly grated
    Parmesan cheese, preferably
    parmigiano-reggiano
About 1 cup homemade chicken stock or
    canned chicken broth, preferably
    low-sodium type
Shredded fresh basil for garnish (optional)

A perennial favorite from my assistant, Ellen Berger-Quan, whose mother, Shirley Berger, developed the recipe many years ago back in her hometown of Philadelphia.

Quickly rinse the chicken under cold running water and pat dry with paper toweling. Cut the chicken into bite-sized pieces.

In a shallow bowl large enough to hold the chicken, beat the eggs. Add the chicken and stir to coat the chicken thoroughly. Set aside for about 15 minutes.

Pour the corn flakes or bread crumbs into a shallow dish. Roll the chicken pieces in the corn flakes or bread crumbs, patting the pieces with your fingertips so that the coating adheres to them.

In a sauté pan or large, heavy skillet, combine the butter and/or oil over medium-high heat. When the butter melts, add the chicken pieces without crowding the pan and brown on all sides. Using a slotted utensil or tongs, transfer the chicken to paper toweling to drain. Cook the remaining chicken in the same manner, adding more butter and/or oil as necessary to prevent sticking.

Preheat an oven to 350° F.

When all of the chicken is browned, arrange about half of it in the bottom of a 9-by-13-inch baking dish. Cover with about half of the mushrooms, olives, and artichokes. Sprinkle with ½ cup of the cheese. Add the remaining chicken, then top with the remaining mushrooms, olives, and artichokes. Sprinkle with about ¼ cup of the remaining cheese. Pour enough chicken stock or broth over the top to reach about halfway up the sides of the dish. Bake until the casserole bubbles, the cheese melts, and the top is lightly browned, about 25 minutes.

Remove the casserole from the oven and sprinkle with the remaining ¾ cup cheese. Serve hot or at room temperature. Sprinkle with the basil just before serving.

SERVES 6.

Spicy Turkey Shepherd's Pie

2 tablespoons canola oil or other
   high-quality vegetable oil
1 cup chopped yellow onion
1 pound ground turkey
8 ounces spicy turkey sausage or hot pork
   sausage, crumbled
1 tablespoon minced fresh thyme, or
   1 teaspoon crumbled dried thyme
¼ cup (½ stick) unsalted butter
2 tablespoons all-purpose flour
¾ cup homemade turkey or chicken stock
   or canned chicken broth, preferably
   low-sodium type
Salt
Freshly ground black pepper

BUTTERMILK MASHED
POTATOES
1 pound potatoes
2 tablespoons unsalted butter
2 tablespoons chopped garlic
About ½ cup buttermilk
Salt
Freshly ground black or white pepper

Snipped fresh chives or garlic chives for
   garnish

Garlic and buttermilk add a welcome tanginess to the traditional topping of mashed potatoes for this old English casserole. Plus, I've come up with a newfangled filling to replace the classic ground lamb mixture.

Boiling or waxy potatoes whip up smooth and creamy; baking potatoes produce a fluffy crown. For a whimsical topping, choose white potatoes, purple potatoes, and yellow varieties or sweet potatoes. Cook, mash, and whip each type separately. Spoon over the top and swirl to marbleize or create desired patterns.

Heat the oil in a sauté pan or skillet over medium heat. Add the onion and cook until soft, about 5 minutes. Add the turkey, sausage, and thyme and cook just until the turkey is opaque, about 5 minutes. Remove from the heat and set aside.

In a medium-sized saucepan, melt the butter over medium heat. Add the flour and cook, stirring or whisking, until smooth and well blended, about 3 minutes; do not brown. Slowly stir or whisk in the stock or broth and cook, stirring almost constantly, until the mixture thickens, 5 to 8 minutes. Stir into the turkey mixture and season to taste with salt and pepper. Set aside.

To make the mashed potatoes, peel the potatoes and cut into pieces of uniform size about ¾ inch thick. Rinse the pieces under cold running water to remove the surface starch. Place the pieces in a saucepan and add water to cover by about 4 inches, then remove the potatoes. Bring the water to a boil over medium-high heat, add the potatoes, and cook until just tender when pierced with a wooden skewer or small, sharp knife, 15 to 20 minutes.

While the potatoes are cooking, heat the butter in a small skillet over medium heat. Add the garlic and sauté until soft, about 1 minute. Add ½ cup buttermilk and heat just until warm. Drain the potatoes, return them to the pan over heat, and shake the pan until the excess moisture evaporates and potatoes are dry to the touch. Press the hot potatoes through a ricer into a large bowl. Stir in the buttermilk mixture and season to taste with salt and pepper. Using a wooden spoon or wire whisk, whip the potatoes until light and fluffy, adding additional warm buttermilk if required to form desired consistency; avoid making the potatoes too thin.

Preheat an oven to 375° F. Spoon the turkey mixture into a 1½- to 2-quart casserole. Spread the mashed potatoes evenly over the top of the turkey mixture. Bake until the turkey is bubbling hot and the potatoes are lightly tinged with brown, about 35 minutes.
SERVES 6.

Asian Eggplant Casserole

2 red sweet peppers
12 slender Asian-type eggplants (about
   3½ pounds)
About ½ cup high-quality vegetable oil
1½ cups finely chopped yellow onion
⅓ cup minced green onion, including
   green portions
3 tablespoons minced fresh ginger root
1 tablespoon minced or pressed garlic
1½ pounds ground lean lamb
1½ pounds ground lean beef
8 dried black mushrooms, soaked in
   warm water to cover for 30 minutes
   until soft, drained, tough stems
   discarded, and finely chopped
1 cup cooked white rice
2 tablespoons Asian sesame oil
⅓ cup soy sauce, preferably tamari
⅓ cup minced fresh cilantro (coriander)
¼ cup plus ⅓ cup hoisin sauce
Freshly ground Sichuan pepper or black
   pepper
¼ cup sesame seed, toasted
Thinly julienned green onion for garnish
Fresh cilantro sprigs for garnish

Greek moussaka was the inspiration for these individually molded casseroles seasoned with the flavors of the Pacific rim.

Place the peppers on a grill rack over a charcoal fire, hold them over a gas flame, or place them under a preheated broiler. Roast, turning several times, until the skin is charred on all sides. Place them in a loosely closed paper bag to cool for 10 to 15 minutes. Remove from the bag and rub away the charred skin with your fingertips. Cut the peppers in half and remove and discard the stems, seeds, and veins. Slice lengthwise into long, thin strips and set aside.

Meanwhile, preheat an oven to 375° F.

Cut off the stem end from the eggplants. Cut each eggplant lengthwise into slices about ¼ inch thick. Brush the slices on each side with oil. Arrange the eggplant slices in a single layer on a baking sheet and bake until tender, 15 to 20 minutes. Remove the eggplant slices from the oven and let them cool until they can be handled. Leave the oven set at 375° F.

While the eggplant slices are cooking, heat 3 tablespoons of the oil in a large sauté pan over medium-high heat. Add the yellow onion, minced green onion, and ginger and sauté until the onion is soft and golden, about 5 minutes. Add the garlic and sauté for 1 minute longer. Add the lamb, beef, and mushrooms and cook, breaking up the meats with a wooden spoon, until the meats are just past the pink stage, 10 to 15 minutes. Stir in the rice, sesame oil, soy sauce, minced cilantro, and ¼ cup of the hoisin sauce. Season to taste with Sichuan or black pepper. Set aside.

Grease six 2-cup baking dishes. Cut 6 rounds of baking parchment large enough to line the bottom and sides of the dishes. Press the rounds into the dishes. Grease the parchment. Line the bottom and sides of the dishes with the eggplant slices, overlapping them slightly. Spoon in the meat mixture level with the top of each dish. Cover with aluminum foil and bake for 30 minutes.

Transfer the baking dishes to a work surface, remove covers, and allow to cool for about 10 minutes. Invert each individual serving dish onto a plate, then carefully remove the dish and parchment liner. Brush the remaining ⅓ cup hoisin sauce over the eggplant casseroles to glaze. Arrange the reserved pepper strips over the eggplant and then sprinkle with the toasted sesame seeds. Garnish with the julienned green onion and cilantro sprigs.

SERVES 6.

South African *Bobotie*

1 thick slice bread
About 1 cup milk
2 tablespoons olive oil
2 cups finely chopped yellow onion
1 pound ground lamb
1 pound ground beef
2 teaspoons coriander seed
2 tablespoons apricot jam or fruit chutney
¼ cup freshly squeezed lemon juice
3 heaping tablespoons Curry Powder
    (page 91) or high-quality commercial
    curry powder
¼ cup slivered blanched almonds
½ cup golden raisins
½ cup halved or quartered dried apricots
5 eggs
Salt
Freshly ground black pepper
Fresh or dried lemon leaves, kafir lime
    leaves, or bay leaves

Stephen Suzman shared this Cape Malay specialty from his homeland. The casserole is usually served with rice cooked with a pinch of saffron or turmeric and toasted coconut. Other appropriate toppings that may be offered include chopped toasted nuts and chutney.

Preheat an oven to 350° F. Grease a 9-by-13-inch casserole and set aside.

Place the bread in a small bowl, add the milk to cover, and let stand until the bread is soft, about 5 minutes.

In a sauté pan or skillet, heat the oil over medium-high heat. Add the onion and sauté until soft but not browned, about 5 minutes. Add the lamb and beef and cook, breaking up the meats with a wooden spoon, until the meats are lightly colored but still a little pink, about 8 minutes. Transfer the mixture to a large mixing bowl.

In a small, heavy skillet, heat the coriander seed over medium heat, stirring or shaking the pan quite frequently, until fragrant, about 3 minutes. Be careful not to burn the seed. Pour onto a plate to cool, then grind to a powder in an electric spice grinder. Set aside.

Squeeze the milk from the soaked bread, reserving the milk. Tear the bread into small pieces and add it to the meat-onion mixture. Add the jam or chutney, lemon juice, curry powder, ground coriander, almonds, raisins, apricots, and 1 of the eggs to the meat mixture and mix lightly but thoroughly. Season to taste with salt and pepper. Spread the mixture in an even layer in the prepared casserole dish. Bake until the meat just begins to brown, about 15 minutes.

Remove the casserole from the oven. Distribute the lemon leaves, kafir lime leaves, or bay leaves over the top of the meat and press them down lightly. Measure the reserved milk and add more, if needed, to equal 1 cup. Break the remaining 4 eggs into a mixing bowl and beat lightly. Add the milk and beat lightly to blend well. Carefully pour the egg mixture over the meat mixture and leaves. Return the casserole to the oven and bake until the custard is set, about 30 minutes.

Remove the casserole from the oven and let stand for about 15 minutes before cutting into squares. Serve warm or at room temperature.
SERVES 6.

Sausage and Pasta Casserole

4 quarts water
10 ounces dried pasta
1 pound bulk hot pork sausage
1 pound bulk mild pork sausage
3 cups chopped yellow onion
½ cup finely chopped green onion, including green portion
1 tablespoon minced or pressed garlic
8 tablespoons (½ cup or 1 stick) unsalted butter
5 tablespoons all-purpose flour
3 cups homemade beef or chicken stock or canned beef or chicken broth, preferably low-sodium type
3 cups freshly shredded Cheddar, fontina, or other smooth-melting cheese (about 10 ounces)
About 2 cups canned evaporated milk
Salt
Freshly ground black pepper
About 2 cups fine dried bread crumbs, preferably from French bread
Minced fresh chives for garnish

My friendship with Ed Broussard dates back to our student days at New Orleans Baptist Theological Seminary. Ed's death, while I was working on this book, reminded me of this dish, which I encountered for the first time a few years ago when I was last privileged to sit down to one of his scrumptious meals. Although Ed used flat egg noodles in the casserole, a mixture of fanciful pasta shapes in assorted flavors adds more color. Ed also used pasteurized cheese, which I must admit makes a smoother version than the white Cheddar or fontina that I recommend here.

Fill a large pot with the water and bring to a rapid boil over high heat. Drop in the pasta and cook, stirring frequently, until al dente. Drain, rinse to remove surface starch, and set aside in a large bowl.

Crumble the sausage in a sauté pan or heavy skillet over medium-high heat. Cook, breaking up the sausage with a wooden spoon, until the sausage begins to brown and renders some of its fat. Add the yellow and green onions and sauté, continuing to break up the sausage, until the onions are soft, about 5 minutes. Add the garlic and sauté for 1 minute longer. Remove from the heat and set aside.

In a saucepan, melt 5 tablespoons of the butter over medium heat. Add the flour and cook, stirring or whisking, until smooth and well blended, about 3 minutes. Slowly stir or whisk in the stock or broth and cook, stirring almost constantly, until the mixture is smooth and thickens to the consistency of heavy (whipping) cream, about 10 minutes. Add the cheese and 2 cups milk and stir until the cheese melts.

Grease a 9-by-13-inch baking dish or a 2-quart casserole. Preheat an oven to 350° F.

Add the sausage mixture and cheese sauce to the bowl with the pasta. Season to taste with salt and pepper. If the mixture seems a bit too thick, add a little more evaporated milk. Transfer the mixture to the prepared baking dish. Sprinkle the bread crumbs evenly over the top. Cut the remaining 3 tablespoons butter into tiny pieces and dot them evenly on top. Bake until bubbly, about 30 minutes.

Serve piping hot. Sprinkle each portion with chives.
SERVES 6.

Smoked Pork and Sauerkraut Casserole

1 pound salt pork, in one piece
1 pound slab bacon, in one piece
3 tablespoons olive oil
1 cup chopped yellow onion
2 pounds sauerkraut, preferably freshly
   made, rinsed and drained
2 teaspoons minced or pressed garlic
2 cups dry white wine
1 cup homemade chicken stock or canned
   chicken broth, preferably low-sodium
   type
1 tablespoon juniper berries, lightly
   crushed
1 teaspoon mixed whole black and white
   peppercorns
3 whole cloves
2 bay leaves
1 pound kielbasa, cut into 6 equal pieces
6 boneless smoked pork chops
1½ pounds small to medium-sized boiling
   potatoes, peeled
6 knackwurst or frankfurters
Minced fresh parsley for garnish

Many versions of this dish, known to the French as *choucroute garnie*, are found in Europe. Serve with German-style mustard or other favorite mustards.

In a saucepan, combine the salt pork, bacon, and just enough water to cover. Bring to a boil over high heat and parboil for 5 minutes. Drain and rinse under running cold water. Set aside.

Preheat an oven to 400° F.

In a sauté pan or heavy skillet, heat the olive oil over medium-high heat. Add the onion and sauté until golden, about 10 minutes. Add the sauerkraut and sauté for 5 minutes longer. Add the garlic and sauté for 1 minute longer. Stir in the wine and stock or broth and transfer the mixture to a 4-quart casserole or other baking dish.

Tie the juniper berries, peppercorns, cloves, and bay leaves in a cheesecloth bag and bury the spice bag, salt pork, and bacon in the sauerkraut. Cover tightly and place in the oven for 3 hours.

Remove the casserole from the oven, uncover, and arrange the kielbasa, pork chops, and potatoes on top of the sauerkraut. Cover and return to the oven for 1 hour.

Meanwhile, place the knackwurst or frankfurters in a saucepan. Add water to cover and remove the knackwurst or frankfurters. Prick the sausages with the tines of a fork. Bring the water to a boil over high heat, then drop the sausages into the boiling water and cook for 1 minute. Remove from the heat and let stand in the hot water.

About 10 minutes before the end of the cooking time, lay the knackwurst or frankfurters on top of the casserole to heat through.

To serve, spoon a portion of the sauerkraut onto each plate. Slice the salt pork, bacon, and sausages, if desired. Arrange the meats and potatoes around the sauerkraut. Sprinkle with the parsley.

SERVES 6.

Cassoulet

2 pounds dried white beans such as
  flageolet, navy, or white kidney
1 yellow onion studded with 4 whole
  cloves
1 tablespoon minced fresh thyme, or
  1 teaspoon crumbled dried thyme
2 bay leaves
Salt
Freshly ground black pepper
1 duck (about 5 pounds)
1 pound boneless lamb leg or shoulder,
  cut into 1-inch cubes
1 pound boneless pork, cut into 1-inch
  cubes
About 4 tablespoons fruity olive oil,
  preferably extra-virgin
1 pound garlic sausage such as Polish
  kielbasa or Italian *cotechino*, skinned
  and sliced about ¾ inch thick
½ pound thickly sliced bacon, chopped
3 cups chopped yellow onion
1 cup chopped carrot
1 tablespoon minced or pressed garlic
4 cups homemade lamb or beef stock or
  canned beef broth, preferably
  low-sodium type
1 cup dry white wine
½ cup fresh or canned tomato purée
2 cups fine dried bread crumbs
½ cup minced fresh parsley, preferably
  flat-leaf type
3 tablespoons unsalted butter or duck fat,
  cut into tiny pieces
Fresh lavender sprigs or parsley sprigs for
  garnish

French cooks continue their long-running disagreement as to which meats should be added to this granddaddy of all casseroles. Some argue that this celebrated peasant dish of southwestern France should contain only pork, others insist on preserved duck or goose (confit), and many add a combination of whatever meats are on hand.

When food and wine consultant Scottie McKinney tested this recipe in her own kitchen on Labor Day, she informed me that it gave a whole new meaning to the holiday. Although cassoulet is time-consuming, it may be done in stages over a couple of days. For example, the beans may be cooked and the duck roasted on one day and refrigerated overnight before continuing. Or the entire casserole can be assembled on the first day and refrigerated overnight, then baked for a couple of hours before serving.

Carefully pick over the beans to remove shriveled beans and grit or other foreign matter. Place in a bowl, cover with cold water, and let stand overnight.

Drain the beans and transfer to a large, heavy saucepan. Add the whole onion, thyme, bay leaves, and water to cover by 3 inches and bring to a boil over high heat. Season lightly with salt and pepper. Reduce the heat to low and simmer until the beans are almost tender, about 45 minutes; skim off any foam that rises to the surface. Drain the beans into a large bowl, reserving the liquid, and discarding the onion and bay leaves. Set aside.

Meanwhile, preheat an oven to 450° F.

Pull off and discard all of the fat from inside the duck. Quickly rinse the duck under cold running water and pat dry with paper toweling. Season lightly inside and out with salt and pepper. Place on a wire rack in a roasting pan. Roast the duck until approximately half cooked, about 40 minutes. Drain off any fat collected in the cavity and set the duck aside.

Quickly rinse the lamb and pork under cold running water and pat dry with paper toweling. Season lightly with salt and pepper.

In a sauté pan or heavy skillet, heat 2 tablespoons of the oil over medium-high heat. Add the lamb and brown on all sides. Using a slotted utensil or tongs, transfer the lamb to a plate. If necessary, add more oil to the pan to equal 2 tablespoons. Add the pork and brown on all sides. Transfer the pork to the plate with the lamb. Set aside. Add the sausage and brown lightly. Transfer the sausage to the plate with the other meats.

→

In a sauté pan or heavy skillet, cook the bacon over medium heat until the fat is rendered. Add the onion and carrot and sauté until the vegetables are soft, about 15 minutes. Add the garlic and sauté for 1 minute longer. Add the stock or broth, wine, and tomato purée. Bring to a boil, then reduce the heat to low and simmer, uncovered, for about 10 minutes. Stir this mixture into the beans and season to taste with salt and pepper.

Skin the duck. Pull the meat off the bones and cut it into large, bite-sized pieces. Set aside.

Preheat an oven to 325° F.

Pour about half of the bean mixture into a 4-quart casserole. Scatter the duck meat and browned lamb, pork, and sausage over the beans. Top with the remaining beans. Add enough of the reserved bean liquid to reach almost to the top of the beans; use a little water or more stock or broth if needed.

In a small bowl, combine the bread crumbs and minced parsley. Sprinkle half of the mixture over the top of the casserole. Bake for about 45 minutes.

Remove the casserole from the oven. Stir the bread-crumb topping into the casserole. Smooth the top and scatter the remaining crumb-parsley mixture over the top. Dot with the butter or duck fat. Return the casserole to the oven and bake until the top is brown and crusty and most of the liquid has cooked away, 45 minutes to 1 hour.

Garnish each portion with herb sprigs.

SERVES 8 TO 10.

BASICS

Here are directions for making ingredients, toppings, and accompaniments that are called for in the preceding stew and casserole recipes. You will find everything here from homemade curry powder to crisp pastry crowns. Since most stews need an accompanying starch, I've also included complete directions for rice, polenta, mashed potatoes, and pasta.

Perfect Rice

Short-grain or pearl rice is soft and tends to stick together when cooked. Long-grain rice cooks up fluffy and the grains remain separated.

1 cup rice
1 tablespoon unsalted butter or high-quality vegetable oil for sautéing
¼ to ½ cup finely chopped yellow onion
1½ to 2½ cups homemade stock, canned broth (preferably low-sodium type), or water
Salt
1 tablespoon unsalted butter for adding to cooked rice (optional)

If using imported rice, spread it out on a tray or flat surface and pick over it by hand to remove any foreign bits or imperfect grains.

To wash the rice, place it in a bowl and add cold water to cover. Stir vigorously with your fingertips, then drain off the water. Repeat this procedure several times until the water runs almost clear. For uniformly cooked, very fluffy rice, transfer the rice to a bowl and soak in water to cover for at least 1 hour or as long as overnight. Drain well.

Heat 1 tablespoon butter or oil in a heavy saucepan over medium-high heat. Add the onion and sauté until soft but not browned, about 5 minutes. Add the drained rice and gently sauté until all the grains are well coated, about 2 minutes.

If using regular white rice, add 1½ cups of the stock, broth, or water and salt to taste. For brown rice, add 2 cups of the selected cooking liquid. For parboiled (converted) rice, add 1½ cups liquid. Bring to a boil, then stir once, reduce the heat to very low, and cover tightly. Simmer white rice for 17 minutes, brown rice for 45 minutes, and follow package directions for cooking parboiled rice. Do not remove the cover or stir during cooking.

Remove white rice from the heat. If any liquid remains in the pot, cover again and place over low heat until the liquid evaporates, 2 to 4 minutes. Turn off the heat under the brown rice and let stand on the warm burner for 10 minutes before removing the cover. Add 1 tablespoon butter (if used) to the finished rice and fluff with a fork, lifting from the bottom instead of stirring, to separate grains gently.

Alternatively, prepare as above but cover tightly and transfer to a preheated 400° F oven just as soon as the liquid boils. Cooking times are the same.

Makes about 3 cups white or parboiled rice, or 3 to 4 cups brown rice; serves 4 to 6.

Wild Rice

Any vegetable or meat stock can be used as the cooking liquid; choose one that goes with your stew. Cooked grains should be al dente and not yet popped open. For a chewy texture, reduce the cooking time; for softer rice, increase the cooking time.

1 cup wild rice
3 cups homemade stock, canned broth (preferably low-sodium type) or water
Salt
1 tablespoon unsalted butter (optional)

Place the rice in a wire strainer and wash thoroughly under running cold water until the water runs clear. Drain.

In a saucepan, bring the stock, broth, or water to a boil over high heat. Add the rice and salt to taste and return to a boil. Stir once, cover, reduce the heat to low, and simmer until just tender, about 35 to 40 minutes. Remove from the heat and drain off any excess water. Cover the pot with a piece of paper toweling, replace the lid, and let stand until the rice is dry, about 4 minutes. Add the butter (if used) and fluff with a fork, lifting from the bottom instead of stirring.

Makes 3½ to 4 cups; serves 4 to 6.

Basic Polenta

Although in the United States we identify Italian cornmeal mush with the coarse yellow cornmeal sold here as polenta, in Italy the type of cornmeal used to make polenta or the softer *polentina* varies with the region. Finely ground yellow or white cornmeal is favored in the Veneto; a coarse yellow meal is preferred in Piedmont and Lombardy. Successful polenta can be made with stone-ground, water-ground, or regular American cornmeal in yellow, white, or even blue or red. Choose a cooking liquid that complements the stew.

2 cups cornmeal (see recipe introduction for type)
1 tablespoon salt, or to taste
10 cups cold water, homemade stock, or canned broth (preferably low-sodium type) for soft *polentina*, or 6 cups cold water, homemade stock, or canned broth for firm polenta

OPTIONAL ADDITIONS
½ cup (1 stick) unsalted butter
⅔ cup freshly grated Parmesan cheese, preferably parmigiano-reggiano
2 cups shredded good-melting cheese such as fontina or crumbled goat's milk cheese
2 tablespoons minced fresh herb of choice, or 2 teaspoons crumbled dried herb of choice
1 cup sautéed fresh wild mushrooms such as chanterelles or porcini
1 cup chopped cooked spinach, Swiss chard, or other greens

In a heavy saucepan or copper polenta pan, combine the cornmeal, salt, and water, stock, or broth; stir well. Place over medium-high heat and bring to a simmer, stirring occasionally with a wooden spoon. Reduce the heat to low and simmer, stirring frequently and scraping the bottom of the pot with the spoon, until done to the soft or firm state described below.

For soft *polentina*, cook until the mixture thickens to the texture of cream of wheat, 25 to 30 minutes; add more liquid if necessary to achieve a smooth, soft consistency. Remove from the heat and, if desired, stir in any one or a compatible combination of the suggested additions. Stir until the butter or cheese melts (if used) and serve immediately. Pour or spoon polenta into shallow bowls and ladle stew over the top. Or transfer the plain *polentina* to the top portion of a double boiler set over simmering water and keep warm; stir in more of the same cooking liquid as needed to keep the mixture pourable until serving time. Just before serving, stir in the chosen additions (if used) and stir until the butter or cheese melts (if used).

For firm polenta, cook until the mixture comes away from the sides of the pan and is thick enough to hold the wooden spoon upright, 35 to 45 minutes. Remove from the heat and, if desired, stir in any one or a compatible combination of the suggested additions. Stir until the butter or cheese melts (if used). Pour the mixture onto a platter or other flat surface and smooth the top with a damp wooden spoon. Alternatively, pour the polenta into a bowl that has been dampened with water, then unmold onto a serving plate. Cut polenta into wedges and serve warm.

Serves 6 to 8.

Mashed Potatoes

Take your choice as to the type of potato to use: boiling or waxy potatoes whip up smooth and creamy; baking potatoes produce a fluffy dish. In either case, avoid using potato mashers or food mills, which break up too many starch-filled cells and cause stickiness. And never subject potatoes to electric beaters or food processors; they'll whip them into glue.

2 pounds potatoes (see recipe
    introduction for type)
¾ cup (1½ sticks) unsalted butter,
    melted and kept warm
About ½ cup heavy (whipping) cream,
    heated
Salt
Freshly ground black or white pepper

Wash the potatoes under running cold water, scrubbing well to remove all traces of soil. Place them in a saucepan and add water to cover by about 4 inches, then remove the potatoes. Alternatively, peel the potatoes, cut into pieces of uniform size about ¾ inch thick, and rinse under running cold water to remove surface starch. Place them in a saucepan and add water to cover by 2 inches, then remove the potatoes.

In either case, bring the water to a boil over medium-high heat, add the potatoes and cook until just tender when pierced with a wooden skewer or small, sharp knife, 35 to 45 minutes for whole potatoes, or 15 to 20 minutes for slices; avoid overcooking. Drain, return the potatoes to the pan over heat, and shake the pan until excess moisture evaporates and potatoes are dry to the touch. As soon as whole potatoes are cool enough to handle, peel and cut into chunks.

Press hot potatoes through a ricer into a large bowl. Stir in the butter, ½ cup cream, and salt and pepper to taste. Using a wooden spoon or wire whisk, whip the potatoes until light and fluffy, adding additional warm cream if required to form desired consistency; avoid making the potatoes too thin.

Serve immediately or keep warm in a partially covered container set over warm (not simmering) water.

Makes about 4 cups; serves 4 to 6.

Pasta or Noodles

A perfect base for juicy stews.

4 quarts water
1 tablespoon salt
1 pound freshly made or dried pasta or
    noodles
About 3 tablespoons unsalted butter,
    melted, or fruity olive oil, preferably
    extra-virgin

Pour the water into a large pot, place over high heat, and bring to a rapid boil. Stir in the salt. Carefully drop the pasta into the boiling water all at once and stir well to separate the pieces. If using long strands of dried pasta, allow the immersed ends to soften before stirring in the remainder. Continue to stir frequently throughout cooking to keep the pasta moving and equally distributed in the water.

Cook until al dente, or tender but still firm to the bite. To test for doneness, quickly remove a piece and take a bite. It should be tender but still slightly resilient. Cooking time varies from about 1 minute for freshly made pasta up to 20 minutes for large dried products. Refer to package directions.

Drain the pasta in a colander positioned over a bowl in the sink. Shake the colander to release excess water, discard water from the bowl, and pour the drained pasta into the warmed bowl. Toss with butter or oil. Serve immediately.

Serves 6 to 8.

Wild Rice Custards

Delicious with any rich meaty stew.

6 cups water
1 cup wild rice
1 bay leaf
1 tablespoon unsalted butter
¾ cup finely chopped yellow onion
3 ounces fresh mushrooms (preferably shiitake, chanterelle, morel, or other wild type), sliced
2 tablespoons minced fresh parsley, preferably flat-leaf type
¼ cup freshly grated Parmesan cheese, preferably parmigiano-reggiano
2¼ cups heavy (whipping) cream
Zest of 1 orange, minced
4 egg yolks
2 whole eggs
About 1 teaspoon salt
About ½ teaspoon freshly ground white pepper
Boiling water, as needed
Thinly julienned fresh orange zest for garnish

In a heavy saucepan, combine the water, rice, and bay leaf over medium-high heat. Bring to a boil, then reduce the heat to medium and cook until the rice is just tender, about 35 minutes; strain to remove any extra water and discard bay leaf. Set rice aside.

In a small sauté pan or skillet, melt the butter over medium heat. Add the onion and mushrooms and sauté until soft, about 5 minutes. Add to the rice. Stir in the parsley and cheese. Set aside.

Preheat an oven to 350° F.

In a small saucepan over low heat, combine the cream with the minced orange zest and heat until warm.

In a mixing bowl, lightly beat together the egg yolks and whole eggs. Strain the warm cream into the eggs and whisk together. Season to taste with salt and pepper.

Butter and flour six 6-ounce soufflé dishes or custard cups. Equally distribute the rice mixture among the dishes, loosely filling each dish about three quarters full. Then evenly divide the cream mixture among the dishes. Place the dishes in a shallow baking pan and add boiling water to the pan to a depth of 1 inch. Cover with aluminum foil and bake until a wooden skewer or knife blade inserted into the center of the custards comes out clean, about 45 minutes.

Remove the custards to a work surface to cool a few minutes. Cover each custard with a plate, invert the plate, and carefully slip off the baking dish. Garnish each custard with the julienned orange zest.

Serves 6.

Caramelized Vegetables

Although intended as an addition to meat stews, this array of slightly sweet vegetables is quite good as a stew on its own. Freely substitute other vegetable combinations, adding them to the pan in the order required for cooking until tender.

¼ cup (½ stick) unsalted butter
2 tablespoons golden brown sugar
3 large carrots, peeled and cut into 2-inch lengths
1 pound baby turnips, peeled, or larger turnips, peeled and cut into 2-inch cubes
Salt
Freshly ground black pepper
1 cup homemade lamb or beef stock, or canned beef broth, preferably low-sodium type
1 pound Brussels sprouts, trimmed, or 1 pound baby zucchini, left whole, or larger zucchini, cut into 2-inch lengths

Preheat an oven to 350° F.

Melt the butter and sugar in an ovenproof pan over medium heat. Add the carrots and turnips and stir to coat well. Season to taste with salt and pepper and add the stock or broth.

Bake, uncovered, for 25 minutes, then stir in the Brussels sprouts or zucchini and bake until no liquid remains and the vegetables are tender, about 15 minutes longer.

Makes about 6 cups; serves 6 as an accompaniment or 3 as a main course.

Black Beans

Included here as the filling for Southwestern Tamale Casserole (page 68), these beans are delicious on their own, or as a side dish with simple meat stews.

Some new strains of black beans do not require soaking prior to cooking. If you know that you have purchased one of those strains, omit the soaking step.

2 cups dried black beans
2 tablespoons olive oil
1 cup chopped yellow onion
1 tablespoon chopped fresh or canned jalapeño or other hot chile, or to taste
2 teaspoons minced or pressed garlic
1 tablespoon minced fresh thyme, or 1 teaspoon crumbled dried thyme
1 tablespoon minced fresh oregano, or 1 teaspoon crumbled dried oregano
1½ teaspoons ground cumin
1 teaspoon ground coriander
About 2 quarts homemade vegetable or chicken stock, reconstituted vegetable bouillon, or canned chicken broth, preferably low-sodium type
2 bay leaves
Salt
Freshly ground black pepper

Carefully pick over the beans to remove any bits of foreign matter or shriveled beans. Place in a large bowl and add cold water to cover by about 3 inches. Let stand overnight.

In a large, heavy saucepan, heat the oil over medium-high heat. Add the onion and chile and sauté until soft, about 5 minutes. Add the garlic, thyme, oregano, cumin, and coriander and sauté for 1 minute longer.

Drain the beans and add them to the pan. Pour in enough stock or broth to cover by about 1 inch. Add the bay leaves and bring the beans to a boil over high heat. Reduce the heat to low, cover, and simmer for 1 hour. Season to taste with salt and pepper and continue simmering until the beans are tender but still hold their shape, about 30 minutes longer.

Use as directed in stew recipe.

Makes about 4 cups; serves 4 to 6.

Curry Powder

Freshly combined curry seasonings usually beat long-stored premixes for flavor. Adjust the amount of peppers to create a mild to fiery mixture according to preference; for mild curry powder, use only half as much peppercorns and pepper flakes.

1½ teaspoons coriander seed
1 teaspoon cumin seed
1 tablespoon ground tumeric
1½ teaspoons cardamom seeds, husks discarded
1½ teaspoons whole black peppercorns
1½ teaspoons dried red chile flakes
1 bay leaf
1 teaspoon whole cloves
1 teaspoon freshly grated nutmeg

Pour the coriander and cumin seeds into a small, heavy skillet over medium heat. Toast, stirring or shaking the pan quite frequently, until fragrant, about 3 minutes. Be careful not to burn the seeds. Pour into an electric spice grinder, mortar, or coffee grinder.

Add the remaining ingredients to the grinder or mortar and grind or crush with a pestle until pulverized. Use immediately, or transfer to a tightly covered container and store for up to several weeks.

Makes about ⅓ cup.

Thai Green Curry Paste

This makes more fiery spice mix than what is needed for a single stew, but it lasts well for several weeks in the refrigerator and has a wide range of uses. Try adding it to soups, pasta sauces, marinades, and salad dressings.

10 small fresh serrano or other green hot chiles
3 medium-sized shallots, coarsely chopped
5 garlic cloves
1 piece (about 1½ inches long) fresh or thawed frozen galangal root or fresh ginger root, peeled and coarsely chopped
1 stalk fresh or dried lemongrass, grassy tops discarded and 3-inch bulb end chopped, or 1 tablespoon freshly grated lemon zest
2 teaspoons freshly grated lime zest
1 teaspoon fresh shrimp paste, or ½ teaspoon anchovy paste
2 teaspoons ground coriander
2 teaspoons freshly grated nutmeg
1 teaspoon ground cumin
1 teaspoon freshly ground black pepper
½ teaspoon ground cloves
½ teaspoon fennel seed
1 teaspoon salt
½ cup chopped fresh cilantro (coriander)
¼ cup high-quality vegetable oil

In a food processor or blender, combine the chiles, shallots, garlic, galangal or ginger, lemongrass or lemon zest, and lime zest in a food processor or blender. Chop until well mixed. Add the shrimp paste or anchovy paste, coriander, nutmeg, cumin, black pepper, cloves, fennel, salt, and cilantro. Purée until well blended. Add the oil, a little at a time, puréeing until smooth.

Transfer to a tightly closed container. Top with a little vegetable oil and store in the refrigerator for up to 4 weeks.

Makes about ¾ cup.

Spicy Cream Cheese Pastry

Use to top any stew for a pot pie. For a plain crust, omit the cayenne. For the stew on page 18, double this recipe if preparing individual pies.

2 cups all-purpose flour
½ teaspoon salt
2 teaspoons ground cayenne pepper
1 cup (2 sticks) unsalted butter, chilled
6 ounces cream cheese, at room temperature

In a bowl, combine the flour, salt, and cayenne pepper and stir together. Using a pastry blender or two knives, cut in the butter and cream cheese to form a soft dough. Alternatively, combine the dry ingredients in a food processor. Add the butter and cream cheese and process with short pulses until the dough just sticks together.

Gather the dough into a ball, enclose in plastic wrap or waxed paper, and chill for at least 30 minutes or for up to several hours.

Makes top crust for 1 large pot pie, or 3 individual pies.

Corn Dumplings

Added on top of a simmering stew, these light dumplings soak up the delicious juices.

1 cup all-purpose flour
1 tablespoon yellow cornmeal
2 teaspoons baking powder
1 teaspoon sugar
½ teaspoon salt
1 tablespoon unsalted butter, well chilled
⅓ cup freshly cut or thawed frozen corn kernels (from about 1 small ear)
⅔ cup milk, well chilled

In a mixing bowl, combine the flour, cornmeal, baking powder, sugar, and salt and mix well. Using a pastry blender or two knives, cut in the butter until the mixture resembles coarse meal. Add the corn and milk and blend until just moistened; do not overbeat.

Alternatively, combine the dry ingredients in the bowl of a food processor. Add the butter and cut in using brief pulses. Add the corn and milk and process just until moistened.

Using a tablespoon, drop the mixture onto a simmering stew, cover, and cook until set, about 10 minutes.

Serves 6.

Ellen's Carrot Cake

This delicately sweet, crumbly cake, created by my assistant Ellen Berger-Quan, is a wonderful foil to spicy stews.

½ cup light brown sugar
3 tablespoons high-quality vegetable oil
1 egg
1¼ cups grated raw carrot (about 6 ounces)
1¼ cups all-purpose flour
⅛ teaspoon salt
1 teaspoon baking powder
1 teaspoon baking soda
2 tablespoons freshly squeezed lemon juice

Grease an 8-inch square baking pan or six 4-ounce baking pans such as brioche tins. Preheat an oven to 350° F.

In a mixing bowl, combine the sugar and oil and beat until creamy. Add the egg and beat well. Add the carrot, flour, salt, baking powder, baking soda, and lemon juice and blend well.

Pour the carrot mixture into the prepared pan(s) and bake until a wooden skewer inserted into the center comes out clean, about 45 minutes for the large pan, or about 30 minutes for the individual pans.

Serves 6.

Phyllo Crowns

If you wish to work ahead, prepare the phyllo toppings and refrigerate them for up to several hours. Bake just before serving and place on top of the stew at the last moment, to keep the flaky dough from becoming soggy.

If using frozen dough, follow package directions for thawing.

About 8 sheets fresh or thawed frozen phyllo dough
About ½ cup (1 stick) unsalted butter, melted

Keep the phyllo dough covered with a lightly dampened towel. Working with a single sheet of dough at a time, cut the phyllo into squares or rounds large enough to cover completely the portion of stew you plan to serve. You will need 30 squares or rounds in all.

Brush 1 phyllo square or round with butter, lay another one on top, and brush it with butter. Continue buttering and stacking to form 6 stacks of 5 layers each.

If prepared ahead, place each stack of phyllo on a baking sheet or tray and refrigerate until a few minutes before serving the stew.

Preheat an oven to 450° F.

Brush the top of each phyllo stack with butter and bake until golden brown, 4 to 5 minutes.

Makes 6 crowns.

Puff Pastry Cutouts

Known to French cooks as *fleurons,* these crisp, golden cutouts are used as fanciful toppings for any stew. Make your own puff pastry dough from a recipe in a reliable basic cookbook or purchase frozen dough. Thaw frozen dough according to package directions.

1 pound homemade or thawed frozen puff pastry
3 tablespoons unsalted butter, melted

Preheat an oven to 350° F.

On a lightly floured work surface, roll out the fresh dough to a rectangle about 20 by 24 inches or spread out thawed dough sheets. Using a sharp knife or rolling pastry cutter, cut the dough into decorative or geometric shapes about 1 inch wide and 2 to 3 inches long. Place the pastry pieces on a greased baking sheet and brush the tops with butter. Bake until the pastry is puffed, crisp, and golden brown, 15 to 20 minutes.

Remove from the oven to a wire rack to cool for about 5 minutes. Use immediately, or cool completely on a rack, then store in an airtight container for up to several days.

Makes 18 small cutouts; enough to serve 6.

RECIPE INDEX

INDEX TO STEW AND CASSEROLE RECIPES IN OTHER JAMES McNAIR COOKBOOKS

ACKNOWLEDGMENTS

Recipes were tested by:

Harvey Berger
Ruth Dosher
Mary Ann Gilderbloom
Gail High
Jim Hildreth
Dorothy Knecht
Debbie Matsumoto
Scottie McKinney
Lucille McNair
Martha McNair
John Richardson
Tom and Nancy Riess
Alice Russell-Shapiro
Kristi Spence
Kathryn Wittenmyer
Sharon Woo

To my publisher Jack Jenson, my editor Bill LeBlond, and the staff at Chronicle Books for their gentle understanding of my personal problems during the production of this book and their willingness to postpone publication to accommodate my schedule.

To Sharon Silva for working extra hours in copyediting to make this book happen.

To Ellen Berger-Quan for her business and personal loyalty, all her hard work to keep me going, and for her beyond-the-call-of-duty assistance in countless ways.

To Diane Quan for all her cutting, chopping, cleaning, and cooking.

To Cleve Gallat at CTA Graphics for turning type and design into a book.

To my extended family and friends who offered so much encouragement and assistance during the difficult months that coincided with putting this book together, especially to Peter Baumgartner, Larry Heller, Gail and Tad High, Dorothy Knecht, Mark Leno, Lucille and J. O. McNair, Martha and Devereux McNair, Peter Olsen, Jack Porter, John Richardson, Richard Snyder, Kristi and Bob Spence, Charles Stinson, Stephen Suzman, Gary Weiss, Felix Wiench, and Barry Wolpa.

To John Carr for the generous loan of half of his home as my temporary photo studio and for the incredible sharing of joys and tears related to Lin's illness during production of this work.

To Addie Prey, Buster Booroo, Joshua J. Chew, Michael T. Wigglebutt, Dweasel Pickle, and Beauregard Ezekiel Valentine for sharing the stews with me during testing and photography.

And to my partner, Lin Cotton, who was physically unable to assist me with this book, but who was the inspiration behind my work. Among my final memories of him will be his quiet little "hummm" when he looked at the plates of stew going to and from the camera.